Conversations with Bob

A Timeless, Entertaining Dialogue for Living an Extraordinary Life

STEVE RIZZO

PEARHOUSE
PRESS
.COM

CONVERSATIONS WITH BOB
A Timeless, Entertaining Dialogue for Living an Extraordinary Life
by Steve Rizzo

Published by Pearhouse Press, Pittsburgh, Pennsylvania
pearhousepress.com

Cover and Book Design: Mike Murray, Pearhouse Productions

Printed in the United States of America

ISBN: 978-1-7347119-9-8
Library of Congress Control Number: 2021917989

This publication is designed to provide accurate and authoritative information in regard to the subject matter covered. It is sold with the understanding that neither the author nor the publisher is not engaged in rendering legal, accounting, or other professional services. If legal advice or other expert assistance is required, the services of a competent professional person should be sought.

Table of Contents

*To my brother Michael, who
taught me how to persevere
through extreme adversity.*

Foreword

The Word According to Bob

*Talent and ability are not the only factors that determine the quality of success and happiness you're going to have. You decide whether you're going to see your life from an advantage or a disadvantage. Only you can choose to shift your thoughts and words to turn challenges into opportunities. All you need to do is connect with your **Inner Bob**. (That's me.) And that's exactly what Steve Rizzo did.*

Steve started writing this book at the lowest point of his life. I'll spare you the details of his downfall, the worst of which was wading through the stages of his divorce after 30 years of marriage.

Steve not only allowed himself to crack open the door to The Negative Zone, he barged right in. That's absolutely the worst thing that could happen to someone who makes a living teaching people how to be successful and happy regardless of their circumstances. Steve is looked upon as an expert in his field. He's supposed to have it together. That's a huge responsibility Steve doesn't take lightly. In his mind he kept thinking that if anyone in life needed to walk the talk, it would be him.

Would you trust a lifeguard who can't swim?

Trust me when I say that an internal war was stirring up between Steve's past, present, and future, between the known and the unknown, and between the negative and positive forces that were battling for control. He was ready to do whatever was needed to make sure the good guys won.

So, Steve decided *(with a little help from me)* to move from his house in Long Island, New York to a rented apartment in Marina Del Rey, California. He was determined to find out who the real Steven Francis Rizzo was, and to find the courage and fortitude to allow inspiration to guide him down a different path.

To relive the internal pressure that comes as a side effect from major life challenges and changes, Steve took long, early morning walks along Venice Beach. With his feet in the sand and the ocean water washing over them, he began to connect with some sort of energy that was outside of his ego, his mind, and his being.

So often on those walks, Steve would fall into deep thought, contemplating where he'd been and where he was going. Sometimes he would allow himself to feel his pain and let the tears fall. Other times he would vent his frustrations and anger, cursing out loud and scaring the crap out of seagulls. But the most profound thing began to happen. Steve found himself constantly engaged in an unusual inner dialogue. (Talking to one's self on Venice Beach isn't all that unusual, but the difference is that Steve wasn't clutching a plastic bag full of empty bottles and cans and wearing only one roller skate.)

It all started one morning with two questions he blurted out loud: *"What the hell am I doing here? What the hell is wrong with me?!"*

Within few seconds came a response, calmly and silently, from within. *"You know why you're here. You know what's wrong. You're just too caught up in your own drama to receive the answer."*

"Wait! What?"

In that moment a serious shift took place. A powerful surge of energy was flowing through Steve's entire body. He immediately turned around and ran back to his apartment, sat at his desk, and began typing on his laptop. Before he knew what was transpiring, a conversation was taking place between himself and *something or someone* on his screen. (*Gee…I wonder who that someone was.*) Steve kept asking questions and allowing for the answers to fill in the blanks.

His early morning walks became ritual, and the dialogue took on a life of its own. Almost without even realizing it, ***Conversations With Bob*** was writing itself.

In this book, you will meet Bob and Bernie.

Bernie is a permanent resident of the negative zone. He resides in everyone, no matter how famous or infamous you are, regardless of race, gender, background, education, religion, or wealth. *Everyone* experiences some degree of Bernie's doubts, fears, anger, and other negative emotions at some point in their lives.

Not only do these Negative Emotions fester inside, but they dictate your perceptions of yourself and your attitude towards life and the people around you.

People unconsciously give their Inner Bernie too much control and power over the choices they make. The scary thing is, they're often not aware of what they're doing to themselves.

That's where **I** come in. Good old Bob! I am of your Higher Nature. I am the ever-present antidote to the firewall of fear that your Inner Bernie insists is real. I also reside in each and every one of you. Always. Right now and forever.

Your mission then, should you choose to accept it, is to force yourself to step away from your Bernie-induced drama and *Woe Is Me* attitude so you can hear the wisdom I have been trying to offer you from my home at the core of your being.

Whoever your Inner Bob is, the trick is to focus on your higher nature rather than defaulting, as so many people do, to ego – or, as I like to call it, the *Big Mouth* inside your head.

Bob is wise. Bob is brilliant. Bob is All-Knowing…And sometimes Bob is really funny! (*I'm not bragging…I'm just saying.*)

Embrace the strategies and secrets that I reveal to Bernie in this book, and you will realize how much power you have over every aspect of your life. It doesn't matter how old you are, how miserable you feel, or how many mistakes you've made.

You… can change your way of being.

You… can experience challenges from a healthier perspective.

You… can actually elevate your overall success and happiness.

You… can choose a better way to live.

I am there for you. I always was and always will be. All you have to do is acknowledge my presence and talk to me. This book will show you how.

Oh…one more thing. If you do choose to accept this mission, you will experience a *Timeless, Entertaining Dialogue for Living an Extraordinary Life.*

Enjoy the process, dear reader.

Peace & Laughter, Bob

One More Thing Before You Start

IT IS MY WISH THAT THE INSIGHTS FROM THIS DIALOGUE, which comes out of one of the most challenging times in my life, will help you to build bridges to a better future. I am confident that the methods offered here will stimulate the spark of hope and creativity that will allow you to implement the simple, internal solutions to turn your life around.

One of the most valuable lessons this book has to offer is that nothing in life is wasted if you view it as a lesson learned. I fervently hope that once you've gone cover to cover you will understand that every step you take, whether forward or backward, is necessary for growth.

Is this a personal book?

YES! It will give you insights, examples, and strategies you can apply to friendships and relationships. It will guide you from victim to victor!

Is this a business book?

YES! It will give you insights, examples, and strategies you can apply to coworkers and customers. It will show you how to persevere with an unstoppable attitude to succeed, regardless of your circumstance!

Is this a life book?

YES! It will give you insights, examples, and strategies you can apply to yourself. It will bring you from down to up. It will bring you from *"woe is me"* to *"wow is me!"*

Is this a religious book?

No! It is not intended as a companion to any denominational (or non-denominational) ideology. It is intended, however, to make you aware that there is a Higher Power within each one of us that we can **converse with, listen to, and learn from.**

Reading *Conversations With Bob* requires (like everything in life) a sense of humor. This, then, is my sincere attempt to use storytelling, humor, and empowerment to help you live an extraordinary life, regardless of your circumstances.

Peace & Laughter,
Steve

Part 1

"The power of Choice is a cornerstone
for Success and Happiness.
There are no ifs, ands or buts about it.
Choose wisely, my friend."
— Bob

*H*ere, we learn how Bernie, a permanent resident of the Negative Zone, winds up in a place where Bob, The One and Only, resides. Their conversation begins, and the bond between the two takes root. And, as the great philosopher Forrest Gump once said, *"That's all I have to say about that."* Happy reading, my friend.

1

A Permanent Resident of the Negative Zone

> "The Negative Zone is like a Do Not Enter Zone for your hopes and dreams."
>
> — STEVE RIZZO

Bernie slid the key card through his hotel room door lock, twice. He sighed and bonked his forehead against the door in frustration. He tried the key again, this time with the magnetic strip facing the other way. Nothing.

Every. Time. Every frigging time this happens to me, he thought.

He flipped the card around again and growled as he jammed it into the lock repeatedly. *"Gaaah!"* he shouted, throwing the key into the air. He stood with his hands on his hips, panting, staring at the key on the floor. After a moment, he bent down, picked it, looked at it and said, "You'd better work this time or I'll tear your tonsils out!" Much to his surprise, the green light flashed, allowing him to enter.

Once inside, Bernie scooted his battered rolling bag into the corner and tossed his laptop satchel on the bed. He was tired. More than that, he was weary. Weary and fed up with the way his life had turned out.

Bernie looked around the room. No surprises. There were never any surprises in rooms like these, except for the ones you didn't want to find.

It was trips like these that brought him down – his internal negative feedback loop was gaining steam once again. Bernie couldn't help himself. It was what he did, night after night, dreary hotel after dreary hotel.

> *"How often do you visit the Negative Zone throughout the day, dear reader? Be honest."*
>
> *– Bob*

While he was only in his early fifties, Bernie looked ten years older. He was convinced that stress had pushed his hairline back way too far, and it was getting harder to hide his balding scalp. He had slipped a bit over time, not the physical specimen he once was, with a thickening middle from too much time sitting on airplanes. For a guy who used to be pretty active, the only exercise he seemed to get now was shoving fast food into his mouth on road trips, and, to top it off, an endless stream of hotel beds had given him a chronic backache. At an age when most men were swimming upstream towards success, Bernie was merely treading water, hoping to make ends meet.

As he kicked off his shoes and rubbed his aching neck, he began to review and recount his personal inventory of injustices and artifacts of negativity, like an obsessive-compulsive person arranging and rearranging his precious collection of useless bottle caps. Dr. Shaw called it "The Oops Loop" and said it could lead to a one-way ticket on "The Pain Train to Frown Town." Bernie typically ignored his ex-wife's therapist's opinion, choosing instead to focus on how incredibly unfair life was and that for the amount of money he was paying the guy could have a better hairpiece.

Bernie believed in honesty, plain and simple. If he sometimes got stuck going over personal failures, he was just telling it like it was. Did he deserve anything less than brutal honesty from himself? No. If he didn't get honest criticism from himself, who would give it to him? No one.

He sat on the bed and thought for a moment about his ex-wife, Elizabeth. They met in an undergrad literature class and ended up in a study group together around mid-semester. He tried to remember what they talked about that sparked her interest.

They sat at a Denny's until the early morning hours, coffee-stained papers littering the table, as they discussed *Death of a Salesman*, the play about a man who has difficulty dealing with his current state and has created a fantasy world to cope with his situation.

"Willy Loman is worried about becoming a loser because he is one," Bernie said. Elizabeth tossed her head back a bit and laughed. "Me, I can't take all that self-pity. He blathers on and on about how he used to be powerful and popular and whatnot, and that now he's a waste of everybody's time. 'The Dream' doesn't just happen, *William*. Try something new, for God's sake, and stop boring *me* to death with *your* death," Bernie insisted.

Even today, Bernie still had very little sympathy for the character. *Cry me a waterfall, old man*, Bernie thought. *At least you had some respect to lose in the first place.*

$$\diamond$$

"This type of pessimistic dialogue destroys any chance at success and happiness."

– Bob

$$\diamond$$

Bernie took off his clothes and ambled into the bathroom. Miniature soap, wrapped so tightly you needed a chainsaw to get at it? Check. Empty, soda can-sized trashcan with no liner? Check. A solitary hair of unknown origin chilling out on the edge of the toilet seat? Was his ex-wife's therapist the last guy in the room? Jeezus.

As Bernie tried to unlock the combination of the shower's hot and cold balance (oddly enough, the only feature that was completely different in every hotel room), he shook his head, grimacing as he waited a good five minutes before the hot water began to kick in.

No one cares, he thought. *No one has any consideration for others. And it's not just strangers, either. Don't even get me started on partnering with friends on business. It's so true what people say. People are awful and awfully stupid.*

As he showered, the negative feedback voice track continued its usual loop.

Sometimes it's the people you thought you were close to that can be the worst, he thought. Not only that, but there's no telling how or when you're gonna get screwed over. And to top it off, most of the time those who succeed don't deserve it!

How is it that Bernie's dumb-as-a-rock brother-in-law managed to sell friggin' camping supplies and find success? Especially since anything Bernie tried failed, sometimes miserably, and they were *all* better ideas *than selling tents and sleeping bags online.* Success was always slipping through his fingers, like the tiny slivers of hotel soaps, or even worse, that crappy biodegradable camping soap Mr. Bigshot cashed in on.

"Jealousy is a Destroyer of the Spirit. Always remember that!"

– *Bob*

He could have taken a slick Wall Street job right out of school. Or done the law school thing like Liz had wanted him to. After a couple of years dueling the other ambitious suits in cubicles, he could have had a cushy office that looked out onto clouds with silver linings, all while he fattened his own golden parachute.

But Bernie wanted more. He wanted to run the show, not just watch it. He would be a business owner, he had concluded, not just some corporate slave. And he did start several businesses. The problem was that he also finished each of them.

Struggling to soap his back, Bernie recounted a mental list of his professional humiliations: the solar panel business, which had left him with a permanently gloomy forecast; the kitchen appliance boondoggle, which seemed to sizzle until it fizzled; the real estate thing with the warehouses in 2008. Oh, brother. He'd stored up enough equity just in time to have the bottom drop clean out from underneath him. It felt like he was always either too early or too late to the party, every single time.

Bernie flopped into bed and flipped the TV on. Channel surfing usually relaxed him enough to climb out of his negativity spiral and fall asleep. At the very least, it often helped to find a reality show that made him feel better about himself.

The normal stuff flashed by on the screen. An old *M*A*S*H* rerun. An infomercial for a device that cuts up vegetables really fast. Bernie stopped when he saw a familiar face.

Oh, please, Bernie thought. He turned up the volume and watched the last ten minutes of a very popular "paid entertainment program" entitled *How to Succeed and Live your Dreams!* He blurted out a low, sarcastic laugh.

"Are you kidding me?" he said out loud to the star of the infomercial, a very tan man with gleaming teeth and blond hair that never moved.

Bernie raised his voice a bit. "I went online, pal! I took your course! I read your books! I have your DVDs, and yes, I prayed! I can't tell you how many times I prayed with my heart and soul! Guess what? It doesn't work! None of it works! I'm no better off now than I was 20 years ago!"

He threw a pillow at the TV in disgust.

"IN FACT, I'M WORSE OFF NOW THAN I EVER WAS!" Bernie shouted.

"I'm sick of being ripped off! And if God does exist – and I seriously doubt it – then I want his email address, because he ain't answering my prayers!"

He turned off the TV and stared up at the darkness. His rage made his body hum and tingle. He could hear the pounding of his heart in his ears.

He was beyond exhausted.

Sleep will help, he thought as he closed his eyes, before speaking to no one in particular. "I guess success and happiness are the luxury of only a fortunate few, and I'm definitely not one of them."

Suddenly, the tingling sensation became a sharp pain in his chest. He tried to sit up, but the pain intensified and immobilized him. Realizing what was happening, he reached for the phone. The receiver clattered to the floor, but with every ounce of strength he could muster, Bernie somehow managed to press '0'. "Hotel Operator. How can I help you?" said the voice on the other end.

In a very low voice, Bernie croaked, "Help! *I need...PLEASE HELP ME!*"

The EMTs charging into the room, the penlight in his eyes, flashes of hotel lobby…all of it blurred together as Bernie slipped in and out of consciousness. In the operating room, the beeping of the heat monitor was erratic. Slowly, the beeps became fewer and farther between.

Bernie opened his eyes. Surgeons and nurses in pressed pastel scrubs were barking instructions back and forth. Bernie felt perfectly calm and wondered why everyone but him seemed agitated.

He sat up, or rather *rose* up, to have a better look at what was going on. Suddenly, he was looking down on himself, as if he was strapped to the ceiling above the glaring operating theater lights. The doctors and nurses feverishly worked even faster trying to resuscitate him.

How can I be here, but see myself there? Bernie thought.

"Hey!" he shouted. "Get me down from here!"

No one seemed to hear him. A ray of white light burst open directly in front of him. He floated into it, sensing he was not alone. Looking up, he noticed transparent figures at the end of what appeared to be a long tunnel, beckoning him to come farther into the light.

"No thanks," Bernie responded mentally to the figures. *"I'll just hang around here for a while. I've seen 'Poltergeist.' There's no way I'm going into the light!"*

His movement was out of his control, however. He tried to fight it, but to no avail. The white light intensified and completely engulfed him. In a split second, he felt himself moving upward at a tremendous speed.

"Hey…What's going on! I told you I want to hang around here for a while. Where are you taking me! Why can't I move! Somebody answer me!"

Trying to make sense of everything, Bernie finally allowed himself to give up all control and murmured, "Well…wherever I'm going, I'm going there fast. At least I'm going up and not down!"

2

I Must Be Dead

> "I fear one day I'll meet God, he'll sneeze, and I won't know what to say."
>
> – RONNIE SHAKES

*I*n a matter of seconds, Bernie's journey upward stops, and the white light that had paralyzed him disappears. Still lying horizontally, he looks around to check out his surroundings. Sure enough, fluffy white clouds stretch as far as he can see.

"Well. I don't know what else I was expecting to see," he says as he's getting up. "It's so beautiful and peaceful." He worries momentarily about falling through the clouds, but his weight is somehow supported.

His attention is immediately drawn to a huge, solid oak door that hovers about six inches off the clouds. As he approaches it, he notices a small, handwritten sign that reads, *"Yes, that's right. You made it. Welcome, Bernie!"*

"That confirms it. I must be dead," he says. He cocks one eyebrow and looks at the door.

"But where the hell am I? Is this heaven? If so, what happened to the Pearly Gates?" Bernie mutters. "I guess budget cuts have no bounds."

Just as he's about to knock on the door, he hears a voice.

"Please wait a moment. I'm out to lunch. I will be with you shortly."

"Oh, isn't this just perfect," Bernie says. "All I did my entire life was wait for something to happen! Now even in death I have to wait! The least they can do is have a waiting room where I can sit and..."

Before he can say another word, Bernie finds himself sitting directly in front of the oak door in a plush, reclining easy chair and holding the latest edition of *AFTER-LIFE* Magazine.

Wow! I better be careful what I say around here, Bernie thinks.

He flips through the pages of the magazine, scanning a few articles. Apparently, Elvis was performing on Saturday, and looking over the "Who Wore It Best?" feature, Bernie decides it's a tie between Mae West and Amy Winehouse.

He looks up when he hears the squeaky sounds of the big oak door opening. Feeling a little nervous, Bernie gets up from the chair and approaches. As he walks through the doorway, he is suddenly greeted by a grinning man who looks like a refugee from the 60s, with long hair tied in a ponytail, earrings in both ears, ripped jeans, worn-out sandals and a t-shirt that reads "HOOF ARTED."

Bernie rolls his eyes. *Great,* he thinks. *If this is heaven, it isn't exactly a highbrow joint.*

"Have you been waiting long?" the man asks.

"I've been waiting my whole life, pal," says Bernie.

"You sound a tad upset."

Bernie shrugs. "It's personal."

"It usually is." The man extends his hand. "Allow me to introduce myself. I'm…"

Bernie raises his hand, interrupting. "When do I get to see the Magnificent One?"

"*Who?*" the man asks.

"*You know, the Light, the Force, the Almighty, The Source Energy, Wonder Woman…The Supreme Being, The Alpha and Omega, Superman, The All-Knowing, All-Being Omniscient Presence…The Creator…of the mess on planet Earth!* Listen pal, I want to talk to GOD! Or whatever they call him…or her…around here."

"It makes no difference to me what you call the Big Kahuna. That's the name most people use here...*The Big Kahuna.*"

Bernie scoffs. "Well, if it makes no *difference*, I'll just call The Kahuna...um... Bob, then."

The man seems thoughtful. He rubs his beard and stares into the distance.

"Bob's a nice name," he finally says. "Just so you know, The Kahuna is neither male nor female, but often appears in a guise or gender that is most relatable to an individual person."

"Whatever...well?" asks Bernie.

The man ignores him, thinking aloud. "Bob. Hmmm...It's short, unassuming. It's a verb, too, which is fun. What do you do when you're lost out at sea? Just, bob, man." He laughs at his little revelation.

Bernie is losing what little patience he has. "*Well*? Where *is* he?"

"Where is who?

Bernie throws his hands in the air. "Bob! I want to talk to Bob!"

"Oh. Well then, go ahead. No one's stopping you. If you want some privacy, I'll be back in a few minutes."

The man turns to walk away.

"No, wait!" Bernie reaches to touch the man's shoulder and takes a deep breath. "Okay...Listen, pal. I want to talk to Bob, but I want to talk in person, face-to-face, in the flesh or whatever form he or she comes in. Do you understand?"

The man nods. "Ooooh... Okay." The man snaps his fingers. He and the door are gone, and Bernie is standing at the end of a very long, winding hallway where the floor is made of yellow bricks.

"You've got to be kidding me," Bernie mutters. "One minute I think I'm in heaven, now I'm in the *Land of Oz*?"

That's when he hears what sounds like children giggling.

"Anybody here?" Bernie shouts. He takes a step towards the other end of the hallway when a little person appears like an apparition from beneath the yellow brick floor.

The little person speaks cheerfully. "Follow the Yellow Brick Floor!" Then, two more little people appear from the walls.

"Follow the Yellow Brick Floor!" they chirp in unison. The strange little people multiply in numbers, now singing along to the tune from *The Wizard of Oz* and dancing around Bernie.

Bernie starts walking, more to escape from what is clearly some kind of hallucination. The little people follow him as he walks slowly onward.

Oh my God! I'm losing my mind, he thinks.

One little person stops in front of him and looks up.

"No, you haven't lost your mind, Bernie!" he says. Another little person bounces up beside the first.

"You've lost your sense of humor and your imagination," she says. They are joined by a third.

"Your patience and your faith and your joy for life," this one says. The first little person steps forward and points at Bernie.

"Your mind *is* next, though." The little people chuckle under their breath.

Bernie replies with a tried-and-true defense: sarcasm. "Thank you. I feel a lot better now."

"No problem!" the little person chirps. "Glad we can help."

"Don't you all have to drop a house on a witch or something?"

Then, with a sweep of his arms to his side, the little person motions to the oak door that is now in front of Bernie.

"Well," he says. "We're here."

"Where's here?" Bernie asks. "Wait a minute. This is the same door that…"

"You wanted to talk to the 'Big Kahuna'…I mean Bob, right?" The little people giggle again.

"Yeah, but…"

"Well, this is his office. This is where you enter, and this is where *we* exit."

The little people begin to slowly bow, walk backwards and disappear into the walls, leaving Bernie standing in silence, gawking at the nameplate on the door…

3

The Big Kahuna

> "Humans, humility and humor; I sure do love what I created!"
>
> – BOB (THE ONE AND ONLY!)

*J*ust as Bernie is about to knock, the door opens, filling his face with brilliant light. As Bernie squints into it, a looming figure steps forward, casting a long shadow over him. Bernie is filled with awe. The light behind the figure is intense and does not reveal the figure's face.

A voice speaks: "Bernie, welcome…oh, man, my bad, let me get the light." The figure claps his hands twice briskly, and immediately the light dims.

Bernie takes a really deep breath and closes his eyes.

When he opens them, much to Bernie's surprise, he now finds himself face to face with none other than the strange, old fugitive from the age of flower power he'd met when he first arrived, *but* he's a lot taller now. His long, gray hair is still pulled back in a ponytail, and his earrings glint a bit in the low light. The only difference is his t-shirt now reads "*Shift Happens.*" Clearly, Bernie doesn't get the joke.

"Come on in, man, make yourself at home," says the stranger, stepping aside.

"You!" says Bernie as he walks in. "What are you doing here? I thought I was going to meet…"

"I tried to introduce myself earlier, but you ignored my gesture and interrupted me. Hi. I'm God. Well, that's what most people call me on your wonderful planet. Or the Magnificent One. Or the Light, or the Force or the Almighty. Or, as they call me here, The Big Kahuna. Or, as you call me, Bob."

Bernie's mouth falls open. "No way," he says. "You've got to be sh… kidding me."

"Yes way." He motions to Bernie to sit. "You're already here, Bern. If you're going to use foul language, why not go for broke? Just be yourself."

"Here?" says Bernie. "Where is here? Am I in heaven?"

"No, you're in Brooklyn." Before Bernie can answer, the man continues. *"JUST KIDDING. Here is where you need to be right now.* Here is where you can discover who you truly are. Here is where you can learn to live the life you so much desire, if you choose."

"Just so you know, dear reader, where you are at any given moment is where you're supposed to be... including reading this book. Please continue."

– Bob

Bernie finds himself seated in a chair on the opposite side of the desk, directly in front of Bob. On one wall, a poster reads "May the SHIFT be with you." On the desk is an old, green-shaded clerk's lamp next to a small page-a-day calendar. The page is marked Mar 9, 12 AD.

Following his gaze, Bob says, "I've been playing catch-up lately."

It finally dawns on Bernie that this isn't a joke or a dream. He's not about to wake up in a strange hotel room, shivering in a feverish sweat.

"OH MY GOD!" he gasps.

"Please, just call me... *Bob.*"

"I'm incredibly sorry. I meant no disrespect before. I just..."

"Not at all. I like the name Bob. Really. It's a simple and honest name. Plus, I believe it makes me more relatable. You know, more accessible, easier to talk to. For the most part, when people pray or talk to me, they have a preconceived idea that I'm someplace far away. Maybe if they were praying to Bob they would feel as if they were talking to a friend, which I am, who is always with them and truly listening, which I am. I think I'm going to use Bob for a while. What do you think, Bernie?"

Bernie just stares as if he can't believe the conversation that's taking place. A hint of a smile crosses Bob's face.

"Of course, that would change a lot of things for folks. For example, when someone sneezes, the response would be 'Bob bless you.' And when people are sworn-in in a court of law: *'Do you promise to tell the truth, the whole truth and nothing but the truth, so help you Bob?'*"

He peeks over the lamp at Bernie, who is still staring at the desk, shell-shocked.

"Oh!" he continues. "What about when people are enjoying a... ya know, shall we say, an intimate moment and scream out my name? *'Oh Bob! Oh Bob! Please don't stop!'*"

Bernie blinks. *This can't be happening,* he thinks.

"Tough crowd. Come on, Bernie, that's funny!"

Bernie seems to snap out of it. "Sorry, it's just so weird. I feel like I'm on *Candid Camera,* or getting punked by some dim celebrity."

Bob laughs and points at Bernie. "No, but I love those shows! And *America's Funniest Videos*! That show kills me! I still watch the repeats. I especially love it when someone is showing off and they screw up! One minute they think they look cool, and in a split second they fall off the stage or ski into a tree!" Bob cackles at this for a few moments. "Humans, humility and humor. I sure do love what I created!"

Bernie is in total amazement. "There is no way that *you* can be God."

"Please, call me Bob. By the way, how did you like the Yellow Brick Floor thing? And the little people? I always liked the idea of everything being controlled by a huckster behind a curtain at the end. I liked that it reminded everyone that they were the ones in control of their lives the whole time."

"So," Bernie asks, "does that mean you're all smoke and mirrors, too?"

"No, my friend. And if I whisked us away somewhere on a tornado, I'd be more likely to take us to a beach resort than Kansas."

"Wow," says Bernie, shaking his head. "God's a comedian!"

"I'll take that as a compliment! Matter of fact, I would include 'comedian' among my top five job titles along with bartender, teacher, nurse and the person at the DMV window."

"Bartender?"

"Woof! The stories I hear!" Bob snorts.

"DMV?"

"Yep. Besides politicians, who gets the most hate directed at them? That job is an unending exercise in forgiveness." Bob grins. Then, his smile fades slightly and he cocks one eyebrow at Bernie.

"So, I will take credit for Laughter. It's without a doubt one of the greatest gifts I gave to humans."

Bernie nods his head.

"Unfortunately, what good is a gift if you don't open it and use it? Except for *Snuggies*. Those are just an abomination."

Bob's comment isn't lost on Bernie. "Hey, I have a sense of humor!"

"No, you *did* have a sense of humor, but through the years it slowly dwindled, along with your imagination and your joy for life. Bernie, you don't use your sense of humor when you need it most. I threw the *Yellow Brick Floor* thing at you just to see if you were paying attention, because we both know that *The Wizard of Oz* was your favorite movie. It always made you laugh, even as an adult. I thought it would lighten you up a bit."

"Humor nips negative thoughts in the bud before emotional havoc blossoms. So, Laugh it off. You owe it to yourself!"

– Bob

Bernie stands up, runs his hand over his head and starts to slowly pace back and forth. He stares for a moment at an hourglass on a shelf in which the levels of sand never change, yet constantly flow.

"Well, maybe I don't feel like laughing," he says. "Maybe I can't lighten up?! Maybe I'm too pissed off and angry! Maybe I feel..."

"Cheated? Ripped off?" Bob interrupts. "Maybe you feel that I let you down?"

Bernie takes a deep breath. He can feel a wave of emotions building. He tries to speak but can't. Then, the tears begin to flow, and there is no holding back.

"You didn't answer my prayers!" he says. "Why? I tried everything! I got down on my knees. I pleaded with you! Do you have any idea of what it feels like to know that you have the talent to succeed, to live your dream and to try everything? I mean *everything*

– only to fall short over and over again? Do you know how difficult it is to watch your friends and everyone in your circle have what you so much desire, to try with your heart and soul not to be bitter or jealous? I've gone through two marriages, made so many sacrifices in my personal life, put so much effort and time into my work, and I have nothing to show for it. I had faith in you. I trusted you. And yes, I'm angry! I'm angry at myself and I'm angry at you! You let me down time and time again. And worst of all...I let myself down. Now I'm dead and it's too late!"

Bernie collapses in a sobbing heap into the chair. Bob sighs. "Whoa, heavy." A moment passes, sand continues to disappear through the funnel.

"Welp!" Bob says, clapping his hands together to get Bernie's attention. "First of all, you're not dead."

"Of course I'm dead!" cries Bernie. "I saw myself on the operating table! I flat-lined for God...for *Your* sake! Wait a minute. Is this a dream? Or a nightmare, maybe. That's it, it's a..."

"Bernie, trust me, you're not dead. And this isn't a dream or a nightmare. Your spirit is just taking a little time off from your body. You can go back to your body and your life whenever you want. That is, if you want."

Bernie looks skeptical. "I can? What do you mean *if* I want? You mean I can choose to go back to my body and continue my life, or stay here?"

"Yes. But before you decide, I thought you would like to talk first. So, I fixed things so we can meet and have a conversation. You did ask for my email address earlier, no? Unfortunately, I don't have one. Kept getting too much spam. And no one except for mortgage lenders has bothered to fax me since 1996." Bob flashes a grin. "What do you say, Bernie? Are you up to it?"

"Do I have a choice?"

"*You always have a choice.* You always did and you always will. That has been one of your biggest problems – not understanding and taking advantage of the power of choice."

"Yeah, well, I always seem to make the wrong choice."

"Well…if you choose to view it that way. That's your choice, too."

"How else can I view it? I screwed up big-time. My life isn't exactly working in my favor. It's the same result over and over again. I feel like Bill Murray in *Groundhog Day,* reliving the same scenario over and over again. Instead of eating pancakes and flirting with Andie MacDowell, I'm falling off the stage and skiing off a cliff."

"Exactly, but haven't you noticed that towards the end of the movie the repetitious scenario stops, and his life finally comes together when he realizes that he can choose another way to live? One choice made the difference. One simple little shift in perspective turned his whole life around. Pretty miraculous, don't you think?"

Bernie shrugs and nods.

Bob says, "A part of your problem is that you're way too hard on yourself. You cannot predict the future. There is no guarantee that the choices you make in the present will turn out in your favor. That's life. *Stuff happens.* Not just to you, but to everyone. You have to use the power of choice to your advantage. In other words, instead of condemning yourself for a choice that didn't work out, why not choose to learn from it and then choose again – until you achieve your desire? Or, better yet, learn the lesson that life is trying to teach you?"

"That's easier said than done," Bernie replies.

"*Everything is easier said than done,*" says Bob. "Just ask any politician. But that doesn't mean it *can't* be done. The key is to never give up. You take your challenges and setbacks personally, Bernie. When you do that, you compound the problem."

Bernie moves to speak, but Bob holds up a hand to stop him.

"I'm not saying that you haven't experienced tough times. Believe me, I've seen *everything*. But you make challenging situations worse than they have to be, because you keep focusing on what isn't working and wailing about how miserable your life is. You leave no room at all in that brain of yours for positive thoughts to seep through. You have become a victim of your circumstances, and victims live in a world of no possibilities. You've created a self-fulfilling prophecy."

"Okay, Bob. So, what do you suggest?"

"Do you really want to know? Do you really want my help? Do you really want to have this conversation? To find out why your life isn't working? Do you want the truth?"

"Yes. Please! I really want to know. I really want – need – to have this conversation!"

"Okay, then. From this point on I'll tell you about how I work, a little on how the laws of the universe work, and then I will teach you some strategies, some skills that will take you to a better place in life. If these strategies seem vaguely familiar to you, it's because the higher part of you already understands this stuff. You were born with it. It's common sense, really. But you've been a permanent resident of the Negative Zone for so long that everything you innately know about success and happiness has been buried."

Bernie shifts uncomfortably in his seat.

"What?" asks Bob.

"Nothing. It's just that…"

"Bernie, relax. This isn't a scolding or a punishment. This isn't brain surgery, either. It's more like brain adjustment. It's a conversation between two friends. Have you ever told a friend the hard truth about themselves? Think of it like that. Your life doesn't seem to be working on any level, and I'm letting you know as a friend why it isn't working. You may feel uncomfortable, but the truth usually is. I'm simply going to teach you the secrets of *shifting your focus* and way of thinking so you can create the life you want…or, at the very least, live a happier, more successful life, both personally and professionally."

"Shifting?" Bernie's eyes flick once again towards the poster on the wall, then Bob's t-shirt. "May the SHIFT be with you. SHIFT happens," he reads aloud.

"Yes, shifting," says Bob. "I was going to use the word 'change,' but that probably would have scared the hell out of you, which isn't such a bad idea, but, I digress. So, I substituted the word 'change' with 'shift.' Shifting your attitude doesn't seem as intimidating a task as changing your attitude."

Bernie nods and chuckles. "Just a few minutes ago you were acting like a comedian, and now you sound like a motivational speaker."

"Not to toot my own horn, but I'm widely considered to be the universe's Ultimate Personal Development Expert. If you doubt my great sense of humor, take a look at some of the characters of *Jersey Shore*, then get back to me. The bottom line is this. I am everything. And I'm here to help you because I care about you. I have all the answers. The added bonus is that my services are free."

Suddenly, Bernie feels very small. "Well, thank you for caring," he says.

"It comes with the job and so are these Common Sense Success Strategies I'm going to be offering from this point on."

"Cool" says Bernie.

Bob suddenly gets very serious. "Oh, my friend, you have no idea. These strategies are way more than cool. They are life-changing. They are real. Very real. They're as valid and true as can be. In fact, these strategies are innate. Everyone on your planet is born with common sense strategies that can guide them through life's trials and tribulations. It's just that most people, for whatever reason, aren't aware that they have them, let alone know how to use them. You may perceive them as trivial, hokey or even ridiculous. But trust me when I say that they are the foundation you need to build your life on."

Bernie straightens up in his chair as if he's buckling up for the roller coaster ride of his life.

Now Bob claps his hands together again and rubs them like he's about to dig into a big meal. "Let's get started," he says with a mischievous grin. "It's time to get your SHIFT together. Because when shift happens, your life changes. At this point you've probably had enough of my shift. I guess you can say I'm full of shift. I apologize – sometimes I'm a real shift-head!"

Bernie rolls his eyes again and says, "*Oh shift*, what have I gotten myself into?!"

4

The Choices You Make

> "I believe that we are solely responsible for our choices, and we have to accept the consequences of every deed, word, and thought throughout our lifetime."
>
> – ELISABETH KUBLER-ROSS

ob leans back into his chair and strokes his chin. "Now, where was I?"

"Choice," says Bernie. "You were talking about the power of choice. I can't believe I have to remind *you* where you were."

Bob grins. "Well, I do have a lot on my plate, you know. After all, I'm the Creator and observer of the entire universe, so give me a break."

"Good point. Maybe I should come back later? Give you some time to get more important things out of the way?"

Bob waves this away. "I can see you've noticed that time has stopped, for a few moments anyway." He gestures at the hourglass on the shelf. "I have that luxury. You do not."

"Well, of course…you're Bob the Almighty…I'm simply Bernie, the one who's half-dead."

"Just so you know, I can be everywhere, conversing with everyone in infinite ways and guises, all at the same time. Well…time as you know it."

Bernie tries to grasp what Bob just said. "You mean right now, as we're having this conversation…you are also in countless other places all over the world…dealing with and listening to…Bob knows how many people, absorbing infinite amounts of information…and with total clarity?"

"Well, I don't want to brag…"

"That's friggin' AMAZING!"

"The first thing you need to understand is that you cannot stop life from throwing crap at you," Bob says. "You cannot stop the unexpected from interfering with your goals and dreams, but you can *always* choose how to respond. You can always choose your state of mind when unexpected challenges come your way. This is a key to your success and happiness in your life."

"For your sake, especially during tough times, get into the habit of choosing positive thoughts and speaking empowering words."

– Bob

Bernie frowns. "I can see that. It's logical. But it's kind of abstract, too. I can smile every time a shovelful of crap gets heaped on my plate, but it won't make eating it any more pleasant, or prevent it from happening again."

Bob shakes his head. "The fact is, your entire life is a result of the choices you make. And for every choice you make, consciously or unconsciously, there is always a consequence. *Always!* In fact, Bernie, here's the hard truth…where you are at this point in your life, personally and professionally, is based on the choices you've made in the past. Those choices are the key factors that determine the quality of life you have right now. There are no ifs, ands, or buts about it."

"That doesn't sound very promising," Bernie says. "Okay, I messed up. I've made wrong choices. I've made mistakes. So, does that mean I have to go on paying the price? Do I have to go on being punished for making wrong choices?"

Bob seems surprised. "Just to be clear, Bernie, I don't punish you. You punish yourself."

"You don't punish people? At all?"

"No. Humans have devised far more effective punishments for themselves than I could ever come up with. Self-enforcing prisons.

Mental and emotional torture they inflict upon themselves, such as guilt, jealousy, anger, self-doubt, fear and a host of other negative emotions. No, my friend, I don't punish and I don't judge. But I do give you countless opportunities to learn from your mistakes, to view them from a healthier perspective and to correct your errors."

"You don't judge people?"

"No, I don't judge. I simply observe, listen to prayers, show the way and guide through countless ways. The rest is pretty much up to the individual. You're not being punished for your mistakes, Bernie. Your life isn't working because of the way you view your mistakes and how you perceive your challenges. You're punishing yourself because you feel hopeless, and you feel hopeless because you don't believe in yourself and in the process of life. And you don't truly believe in me, because you don't know how I operate or how the laws of the universe work."

"I see," says Bernie. "I'm my own worst mental enemy. Anything else?"

"Yeah. You give up too easily."

Bernie throws his hands up. "I can't help it if life keeps throwing me dead ends!"

"Let me reply to that by asking you a question. When you're driving your car and you come to a dead end, what's the next logical choice to make?"

Bernie thinks for a second. "Besides making sure that I'm not being surrounded by zombies? Recalculate my GPS system, choose an alternate route, turn around and move in that direction."

"Exactly! It doesn't make sense to just sit in your car and whine. You simply choose another way to your destination, whatever or wherever that may be – and if that doesn't work, you choose another way. And you keep choosing until you get to where you want to go."

"So, a dead end is life's way of saying 'please choose another way'?"

"Absolutely! Unless, of course, you choose to view it as a dead end. Then you're left with a different set of circumstances." Bob leans forward suddenly and says, "Bernie, pay close attention here. I want you to get this. Adversity isn't a punishment. If anything, it's a blessing."

"*Adversity is a blessing?* Now we're in illogical territory again. Millions of people pray for blessings every day, and what I'm hearing is that they're going to be heaped with even more garbage."

"When people pray for blessings, they should pray to be helped along the way. In other words, my friend, a prayer for a blessing or for a better life is not asking that a particular situation be different – rather, it's asking that you *see* it differently as you work your way through it. Are you following me?"

"I'm following you, Bob," says Bernie.

Bob continues. "Adversity is necessary in order for you to grow. You were put on Earth to experience, learn, grow and become the person you are meant to be. Adversity is necessary for any advancement. Mistakes, defeat, sickness, disasters, divorce, war, death, elevator music, traffic, in-laws, annoying and difficult people and situations. I can go on and on, but I think you get my point. It's all there to challenge you to realize your capabilities."

"Well, that explains a lot," says Bernie.

"It can't be stressed enough that the filter you view experience through ultimately determines who you become," Bob says. "In other words, how you choose to experience what happens to you, be it good or bad, will determine what you learn. What you learn determines how you grow, and this continued growth is what shapes who and what you become. Your job, Bernie, *your responsibility*, is to become the best person you can be. If you can comprehend this, it will help free you from feeling victimized when times are tough, and just maybe help you to consider a challenging situation as a pop quiz in Life 101, rather than, say, the zombie apocalypse."

Bernie nods. "I get that. But to some people, a pop quiz *is* the apocalypse. It is the end of *their* world, at least. I mean…what about the parents who lose their children in a car accident or to an illness? What about the families who receive a telegram informing them that their son or daughter was killed in action on the battlefield? I can turn on the news at any time and witness horrific acts of violence – natural disasters and manmade catastrophes. The list goes on and on."

Bob stands up and walks over to peer at the hourglass on the shelf. When he speaks again, he isn't looking at Bernie, but at the sand grains slipping away.

"Dealing with pain and loss is all a part of being human, Bernie. There is no escaping that. Yet, the truth is that throughout history, even amid the most devastating of circumstances, people have made courageous choices that have not only allowed themselves at least some degree of relief from their suffering, but have led many to become victorious thought leaders who set a higher standard for the rest of the world to learn from."

Bernie sighs and sits back. "Okay, I get it."

"Are you sure?"

"Yes, I'm sure, but…*never mind.*"

"This is a safe place. The safest, in fact. Say what you feel."

Bernie cracks his knuckles and laces his fingers together on the desktop. "So, my misfortune is all on me? Where do you come in? Just a few moments ago, you said that you observe, answer prayers and show the way and guide."

"Yes, I did."

"The fact is, Bob, I prayed and you didn't answer. I don't recall being shown the way or being guided."

Bob smiles and rubs his hands together. "Ha! Now we're getting to the core of the problem. *Your problem.* Yes, you prayed. But the problem is that you pray with the same woe-is-me attitude you have about your business and your entire life. What do you expect, a miracle?"

"Are you kidding me? Of course, I expect a miracle. Isn't that what you're *supposed* to do?"

"How does the saying go? The only thing I'm *supposed* to do is pay my taxes and die, right? As you can see, I do neither, though the IRS won't stop trying."

Bernie smirks and gives Bob an *oh-boy-don't-I-know-it face*. Bob carries right along.

Make the SHIFT

"Right now, your life is being dominated by thoughts of lack, doubt, uncertainty and fear. Your life and career will only change when you change the way you think and feel. Your greatest power to change your life lies in the power you have to seek solutions. *That's a miracle, Bernie.* A miracle can be as simple as a shift in perception that rearranges your life for the better. It's a way of thinking that taps into a higher *possible you* that can change how you view life – which, in turn, will change how life treats you. As long as you keep thinking in limiting ways that define and reinforce the *impossible you,* you will never be able to experience the miracles I have in store for you. I can set up the miracle. I can plant the seed. I can open the door to opportunity, but *you* have to see it as such. You have to make the shift."

"Be Still...and know that I am Bob!"

– Bob

"Make the shift?" Bernie questions.

"There is no greater miracle than the awakening and transformation of a person becoming all that she or he can be," Bob says. "That's their choice and responsibility."

"So, it's my choice. My responsibility. Once again, you have *nothing* to do with it?"

"Okay, listen. You've heard the saying 'God helps those who help themselves?'"

"Yes, of course."

"Have you ever given any thought to what it means?"

"Not really. I figured it had something to do with not having heartburn after hitting up the Chinese buffet."

Bob gives Bernie a smirk. "I assure you, fortune cookies are not my preferred method of delivering a message. Dumpling distress or no, it means that I can only do for you what you are willing to do for yourself. You have to meet me halfway. At various times throughout your life, you have prayed for opportunities and success, and I sent opportunities your way in the form of seed possibilities. But you stopped the seed possibility from taking root with your negative attitude and your woe-is-me stories. Together, we can perform miracles, but sometimes you make it really difficult for me to help you do so."

"Ouch!" says Bernie. "Couldn't you sugarcoat it just a little?"

"You wanted the truth. I delivered it. There's a reason they call it the 'bitter truth.'"

"Point taken. By the way, how can anything be impossible or difficult for you? You're God…or Bob the Almighty!"

"I told you, I gave up direct intervention thousands of years ago. *Deus ex machina* is no fun for anybody in the audience."

Bernie stares at Bob. "Day-oos ex huh?"

"It's Latin for '*God in the machine*,'" Bob says. "It refers to a plot crutch used way back when Greek playwrights didn't have to worry about critics. A character gets himself into an impossible, sticky situation, takes no responsibilities for his choices or actions and blames the Gods for his plight. Or, boom, a God comes down from the sky and fixes everything. Lazy writing, if you ask me. I prefer Grisham."

"But you do have rules?" asks Bernie.

"I wouldn't call them rules. I'd say it's more of a structure that makes good on the first promise I ever made."

BOB's

High Points to Remember

Your place at this point in your life is based on the choices you've made in the past. Those choices are the key factors that determine the quality of life you have right now. There are no ifs ands or buts about it.

You cannot stop the unexpected from interfering with your goals and dreams, but you can always choose how to respond. You can always choose the state of mind you need to be in when unexpected challenges come your way.

As long as you keep thinking in limiting ways that define and reinforce the impossible you, you will never be able to experience the miracles I have in store for you. I can set up the miracle. I can plant the seed. I can open the door to opportunity, but you have to see it as such. You have to make the shift.

Part 2

"You attract to your life anything
you give your thoughts, energy, focus,
feelings, intention and attention to —
whether you want it or not."

— *Bob*

Bernie learns that Universal Laws, which cannot be denied, apply to everyone. No exceptions! Bob reveals to him that there is more to the Law of Attraction than *"what you think is what you get."* There are invaluable *Intangibles* at play.

5

The Law

"*T*he first promise *EVER*? That sounds like pretty important stuff," Bernie says quietly.

"It is important, but most people have forgotten it," Bob replies. "Do you remember what it is, Bernie?" Seeing that Bernie is struggling with what he is being offered, Bob speaks up. "I'll give you a hint, FREE… *fill in the blank…*"

"Free Willy?" Bob quips.

"THE ANSWER IS FREE WILL! FREE WILL! FREE WILL!"

Bernie is pushed back a bit from the force of Bob's delivery.

"Okay, listen," Bob continues. "There are certain Universal Laws that exist that cannot be denied, and they apply to everyone. I mean *everyone*! No exceptions – You, the Pope, John Stamos, whomever. The most important of these laws is the Law of Cause and Effect. Or what most people now refer to as the Law of Attraction."

Bernie nods impatiently. "Ah, I read all about that."

Bob just smirks and sarcastically says, "How's that working for you?"

"What do you mean?"

"Let's just say that reading about it in a few quick-fix books and living your life in accordance with the way it truly works are two totally different things. The phrase 'Law of Attraction' has been misused and misrepresented by far too many so-called experts. However, because it's a phrase that best describes how the Law really works, and for the purpose of this conversation, I'm going to continue to refer to the phrase 'Law of Attraction' throughout. Okay?"

Bernie nods. "I find that an attractive idea."

"If you truly understand how this most powerful law works and live your life accordingly, it can have a dramatic effect on your level of success and quality of happiness. I could get detailed on the quantum nature of why this law exists, but that's probably not necessary for now."

Bernie shrugs. "How about just the CliffsNotes?"

"Good call. It'll give you just enough to pass the test at the end."

"Wait!" says Bernie. "There's a test?"

Bob laughs. "Got ya, didn't I?"

Bernie sighs and relaxes his tensed face.

"Simply stated, you attract to your life anything you give your thoughts, energy, focus, feelings, intention and attention to – whether you want it in your life or don't want it in your life. What you think about and say out loud are what you create, and what you radiate is what you get back."

"I get that," says Bernie. "Like attracts like. I've heard that before."

"Right. This entire universe, including your thoughts, beliefs, feelings, emotions and attitude, are made of energy that moves at specific vibrational frequencies. Everything you experience in your life is attracted to you because the universe – *one of my personal favorite inventions, by the way* – is responding to the thoughts you are putting out there."

> **"Successful, happy people know without a doubt that they become what they think about day in and day out."**
>
> – *Bob*

Bob looks at Bernie.

"I'm following you," Bernie says.

"What you consistently think about or focus on is bound to expand. If you consistently focus on the negative, you will call forth more negative. If you consistently focus on the positive, you will call forth more positive. Your thoughts, words and beliefs, along with the feelings and emotions they elicit, all produce different kinds of vibrations. Positive thoughts are high-energy. They have a high vibrational frequency, which means they move at a faster rate. Negative thoughts have a low vibrational frequency that move at a slower rate. Now, imagine yourself as a human magnet attracting everything you want in life. So, tell me what you're thinking."

"I'm thinking…Come on, ten million dollars!" Bernie shouts. "Come to Papa!"

Bob laughs but shakes his head. "Sorry, Papa. It doesn't work that way."

"Well, you said what you think about is what you get, so why shouldn't I be able to lock myself into a room, thinking and chanting that I have 'millions, millions, millions,' and get rich? I was always skeptical of the 'like attracts like' mentality."

Bob says, "I know you have been, Bernie. Most people are skeptical. Trust me here. It takes a continuous series of high-powered thoughts, feelings, emotions and intention over time to attract the things you want to manifest in your life. This is not only spiritual law, but science, my man. Your brain's job is to be focused and efficient. Only you can make that happen. You want to create well-worn pathways through your neurons to travel faster to my energy field. You can customize your own brain to seek out relationships, ways to overcome obstacles and opportunities to act on just by thinking high-energy thoughts about the same things over and over."

"Wait," says Bernie. "You're saying I can hack my own brain?"

"I'll put it this way," says Bob. "The more you think and feel similar thoughts and feelings, the more emotionally charged you will get, and the more powerful the magnet becomes. It's more like brain training than a brain hack. This is where you have to be careful – matter of fact, it's where most people screw up."

"How so?" Bernie asks.

"Because they don't realize they are *also* attracting the things they don't want. In other words, Bernie, if you are continuously thinking about how you're not rich, and if you are always focusing on what you don't have, you will only attract more of what you don't want."

"I see," says Bernie. "So, then all I have to do is focus on what I want. Right?"

"*Well…not really,*" says Bob. "I'd rather you come from a state of 'having it.' In other words, when you desire something, don't focus on 'wanting it.'"

Bernie gets up and takes a deep breath. His eyes meander around the room again, and he reflexively looks at his wrist. This is what he typically does to buy time when he is confused. The watch is not there. *I guess time isn't a commodity that needs to be bought here*, he thinks. Finally, he speaks.

"Why? You said that thinking of what I *don't* want will only bring me more of what I don't want. So, why shouldn't I just think about what I *do* want?"

"I can see how that's logical for you. But here's the thing, Bernie. By thinking of what you want you are also simultaneously (and unconsciously) thinking that you don't have it yet in your world, which signifies *lack*. Remember, every thought you have is transmitted into the universe. *Everything.*"

Bernie snaps his fingers and sits down again quickly.

"Oh! I get it! The *way* I think about what I want to manifest in my world can also simultaneously send vibrational energy of what I *don't* have into the universe, and by doing that I run the risk of creating more of what I don't have!"

Bob claps. "You got it!"

Bernie is getting excited. "So, if I'm focusing on wanting a new car, and I think to myself, 'I wish I had a better car because my goofball neighbor, Larry, just got a new Audi and I deserve at least that, too, because my crappy old car isn't good enough,' that negative energy is also being delivered to the universe!"

"That's right," says Bob. "And what that does is cause conflict within the energy field, and it really slows down the transmission process, depending upon what you're focusing your attention on most – the new car or the piece of crap. That transmission of frequencies is called 'manifestation.'"

"Okay," says Bernie. "I'm still following you."

"It's important to know that this entire transmission and manifestation process affects every aspect of your life. In other words, the more you focus on your lack, the more of that you'll get back. The more you focus on what isn't working, the more your life won't work, and the more hectic it becomes. When you focus on what is working and what you're grateful for, life becomes easier and opportunities begin to flourish. The more you…well…I think you get my point."

> *"If you think you're an Idiot, you're right… even if it isn't true."*
>
> *– Bob*

Bernie nods slowly. "Okay. So, what do I do? How do I make this manifestation thing work *for* me and not *against* me?"

"Although thinking of what you *want* is a little more conducive to manifesting your desires than thinking of what you *don't* want, the absolute best way to manifest what you desire is to let go of wanting in the first place. Do you understand?"

Bernie looks at Bob and scrunches up his nose. "Sorry if I take a little time to wrap my head around it."

"Take a big time, if you want," says Bob. He points at the hourglass. "I've got plenty of it."

Bob leans back in his wooden office chair and props his flip-flopped feet onto the corner of the desk.

Imagination Encircles the World

"Okay," Bob says. "A better way to manifest the things you desire would be to use your imagination and visualize yourself experiencing what you want as if you already have it."

"Use my imagination...as if I already have it?" Bernie asks.

"Yes," says Bob. "If you want a desire fulfilled in your life – the kind of person you would like to become, or manifest a dream or an idea – the first step is to imagine it. You see, Bernie, your imagination is able to create all that you ask depending upon the degree of your attention."

"Didn't Einstein say something about imagination?" asks Bernie.

"Yes, he did," says Bob. "Einstein said that *imagination is more important than knowledge. Knowledge is limited. Imagination encircles the world.*"

"Wow!" says Bernie.

"It can encircle your world! You can make a future dream a present reality by using your imagination and assuming the feeling that you already have what you desire."

Bernie contemplates what Bob is suggesting. "You know, Bob, years ago I was watching Oprah and heard actor/comedian Jim Carrey saying something to that effect."

Bob jumps up from his chair and says, "Exactly! Jim Carrey is a perfect example of what I'm conveying to you! Before he became a huge star, he actually believed and acted as if he already had the things he desired. On a continual basis, he would imagine, think and say to himself *I already have these things. I just haven't accessed them yet.* In fact, he even went as far as to write out a check to himself in 1990 in the amount of ten million dollars 'for acting services rendered.' He dated the check "Thanksgiving 1995," then folded it up and put it in his wallet. He was certain he was going to make that much money for services rendered in his chosen field. Five years later, a few days before Thanksgiving 1995, he was told he was going to earn ten million dollars for the movie *Dumb and Dumber.*"

> ## "If you can Visualize it in your Mind...
> ## Feel it in your Heart...and Believe that it is so...
> ## You will See it in your World."
>
> ## – Bob

"Now that's confidence!" says Bernie.

"It's more than confidence, Bernie," Bob replies. "It's an unshakable faith. Jim Carrey believed without a doubt that the things he desired were going to come to him, and he acted like they were. He confidently moved forward with his life in order to draw his desires to himself in such a way that his actions were in alignment with what he said he believed."

Bernie thinks for a few seconds. "So, his degree of attention must have been very powerful."

"Absolutely," says Bob. "Your degree of attention *and* intention is crucial. It's the fuel that drives your imagination."

Bernie jumps in excitedly. "And your imagination is the first step for a desire fulfilled, and that's why your degree of attention cannot be underestimated."

"Right again, my smart friend," says Bob. "You should always be aware on a daily basis of the degree of attention and intention you are placing on your desires. Whatever they may be. The more attention and intention you give to your desires, the more powerful the manifestation process."

Bernie thinks for a moment about what Bob has just said. "So… in other words…imagine my desires with a high degree of attention, think and visualize big…live in the belief and the feeling of being the person I would like to become and the things I want to attract…and act accordingly."

Bob's feet hit the floor with a thump as he leans in with a smile. "Yes! Exactly."

B⛰B's

High Points to Remember

Simply stated, you attract to your life anything you give your thoughts, energy, focus, feelings, intention and attention to – whether you want it in your life or don't want it in your life."

The more you focus on your lack, the more of that you'll get back. The more you focus on what isn't working, the more your life won't work. When you focus on what is working and what you're grateful for, life becomes easier, and opportunities begin to flourish."

You can make a future dream a present reality by using your imagination and assuming the feeling that you already have what you desire."

6

Take Action

> "The way to get started
> is to quit talking
> and begin doing."
>
> – WALT DISNEY

*B*ernie feels good that Bob is excited about his answer. "I read somewhere once that the vibrations of thoughts and the emotions they generate can actually be recorded scientifically," he says.

Bob nods. "Yeah, you read that in May of 1981, in *From Enigma to Science,* by George W. Meek. "

"That's right!" Bernie starts to think back to the details. "Wait a minute! How do you know I read that?"

"I know you said it would take a little time to wrap your head around some stuff, but, really…"

"So, you know everything I've read…and everything I've watched?"

"Yep," says Bob. He bursts out laughing. "And every voicemail you've left, and everything you've microwaved at two in the morning. Everything!"

Bernie rubs his forehead, which is turning bright red. "Okay. Everything…this is embarrassing."

"Relax, Bernie. I'm not judging you. I told you I don't judge."

"Okay, thanks," says Bernie. "I'm not trying to change the subject, but can we talk a little more about the Law of Attraction?"

"Certainly." Bob snaps his fingers, and an old rolling chalkboard like Bernie remembers from elementary school wheels up from nowhere behind him. As Bob continues speaking, a piece of chalk levitates and begins writing the word *Attraction*. "Have you ever noticed that the last six letters of *Attraction* spell *Action*?" The chalk magically underlines that portion for extra emphasis. Which implies that you have to do your part. I cannot stress this enough! In other words, not only is it important to think, feel, and visualize the things you desire, but you have a responsibility to take the appropriate action in accordance with the law. This, again, is where a lot of people screw up. This is also where many books on the Law of Attraction failed to make this most crucial point."

"What do you mean?" Bernie asks.

"You can't just imagine, think, feel, and visualize about becoming a doctor and then wake up one day and expect to see patients. That's ridiculous, of course. It takes many years of college, then medical school, countless hours of intense studying, and hard work to become a doctor. There is always a step-by-step process involved."

"Well, that makes sense."

"It's common sense, Bernie. Einstein said, '*nothing changes unless something moves*.' Well, you have to get up off your ass and move! You have to take some kind of action with high-powered thoughts! It's part of the manifestation process. Maybe the first step is just a simple matter of setting up an interview that can lead to your dream job. Maybe it's asking someone for help to achieve a specific goal or taking the initiative to sign up for a fitness program to get in shape. Each step leads to another step. And each step adds to the overall degree of attention you give to your desire."

"I get your point, Bob. Take action. One step at a time."

"Yes, and have no doubt that there will be obstacles and mistakes along the way. Sometimes it will seem like your entire world is falling apart around you. But if you expect to succeed, you have to maintain the emotional fortitude to learn from life's trials and tribulations and forge ahead no matter how severe they are. That's why you must make certain that you keep your thoughts, beliefs, and emotions in sync with my energy field every step of the way."

> *"Dreams without perseverance will*
> *simply remain…dreams."*
>
> *– Bob*

Bernie stares at Bob and feels the intensity in his voice.

Bob sits back down in his chair and puts his hands flat on top of the desk. There is a moment of silence as he leans forward and, in a low but stern voice, says, "Bernie, *you truly are the creator of your success and happiness.* You need to understand in a most profound way that *you are the only problem that you will ever have,* and somewhere within you there is ALWAYS a solution waiting to be discovered."

"I'm with you, Bob."

Bob continues. "Whenever you are confronted with a problem or challenge of any kind, it's never a matter of managing the situation. *It's always a matter of how you manage your mind.* Can you manage your mind and the toxic thoughts and emotions that are keeping you from finding the solution and from living the life you desire?"

"And that's always my choice. Right, Bob?"

"Yes," says Bob. "You can choose thoughts that will lead you to bounce back and become the victor, *or* that will lead you to give up and become the victim."

For a few moments, Bernie contemplates what Bob has said. "Victor or victim…it sure is amazing the power I have over my life."

"Yes, it is, Bernie. Yes, it is…oh, and one more thing. And this is the thing that people find most difficult."

"Oh, we haven't gotten to the hard part yet?"

"Well, it's an intangible strategy and a crucial element for success and happiness that can significantly speed up the manifestation process."

"Okay," says Bernie. "Let me have it."

"I can't stress enough how important this is."

"Important, right." Bernie nods.

"It's the most important part, but people tend to leave it by the wayside. You know how people tend to cut corners? Like when they're roasting a turkey and they forget to brine it beforehand or baste it while they…"

"Bob, please!" Bernie interrupts. "Just tell me what it is!"

"You really should practice patience, Bernie."

"You really should practice getting to the point, *Bob*."

"Okay," says Bob, chuckling. "Here it is."

Bernie's eyes are fixated on the chalk zooming across the board as he listens. As Bob speaks, the chalk writes: *"Make a conscious choice every day to enjoy yourself during the process of whatever you are trying to achieve."*

"Really? That's it?" says Bernie. "Enjoy the process?"

A broad grin breaks across Bob's face, and he says, simply, "Yep."

B🗻B's

High Points to Remember

*E*instein said, 'nothing changes unless something moves.' Well, you have to get up off your ass and move! You have to take some kind of action with high-powered thoughts! It's part of the manifestation process.

*I*f you expect to succeed in life, you have to maintain the emotional fortitude to learn from life's trials and tribulations and forge ahead no matter how severe they are. That's why you must make certain that you keep your thoughts, beliefs, and emotions are in sync with my energy field every step of the way.

*W*henever you are confronted with a problem or challenge of any kind, it's never a matter of managing the situation. It's always a matter of how you manage your mind. Can you manage your mind and the toxic thoughts and emotions that are trying to keep you from living the life you desire?

7

Enjoy the Process

"I just go to my office to enjoy myself; work automatically happens."

– JITENDRA ATTRA

"*S*o, let me get this straight," Bernie says. "You want me to enjoy the process even when I have no idea what's going on or how it will turn out, and it looks like everything is falling apart?"

"That would be 'YEP' #2," Bob says. "Unfortunately, this is something that most people leave out or forget, especially when things aren't working out the way they want. That's when the stress level gets really intense, and self-doubt, overwhelming anger and fear can become very dangerous mindsets. And, without realizing it, enjoyment becomes secondary at a time when it's most important and should be primary."

Bernie just stares at Bob, who has now come to recognize that blank stare as a sign to continue explaining what appears to be unexplainable.

"When you make a conscious choice to enjoy yourself during the process of achieving your goal, you become more creative, more productive, more resilient, and you find solutions to problems a lot quicker. That's a promise, my friend."

"But how? I mean, I see how someone can enjoy themselves when things are running smoothly, but how can a person enjoy the process when nothing – I mean nothing – is working? There are a lot of people who face major challenges every day, Bob. And you're telling me they have to muster up enough courage and positivity to not only move forward, but to be happy and enjoy the process? That's a lot to ask."

"It may sound like a lot to ask. Then again, I'm not asking. I'm just telling you how it works. When you think of the benefits of enjoying yourself and then think of the consequences if you're not, it is well worth it."

"What benefits? What consequences?" Bernie asks. "Why is enjoyment so important?"

"Because seeking the joy that life has to offer generates a massive amount of positive energy. Do you know what that energy manifests into?"

"No," Bernie replies. "But I have a strong feeling that it's not global warming."

"It manifests into passion and enthusiasm. These two forces are key to creating the things you desire. Because the energy they radiate will not only increase your overall degree of attention, but also generate a powerful connection to me and my energy field. In fact, the word *Enthusiasm* comes from the Greek word *'entheos.'* Meaning the God within. Or, in this case, the Bob within."

Bernie chuckles. "Good one, Bob."

Bob smiles, but then stares gravely at Bernie. "Always remember this, Bernie."

Bernie straightens up in his chair. "Funny. You're the most intense when you talk about things like relaxation and enjoyment. So serious!"

"As a heart attack," Bob deadpans.

Bernie takes a deep breath and nods.

The chalk moves back into position and begins writing as Bob recites, *"Enjoyment is the spark that ignites Passion and Enthusiasm.* In fact, Abraham Lincoln was known to say, *'People are about as happy as they make up their minds to be.'* And this was coming from a man who was dealing with an entire fractured country, had to witness the death of two of his children, and whose wife who was clinically depressed."

Bernie takes a moment to consider this. "Are you trying to tell me that happiness is a choice? That I can actually choose to enjoy myself during the process of achieving my goals, regardless of my circumstances? Really? I've heard that before, Bob, and to tell you the truth, I was never a big believer of that philosophy."

"Yes, I know. And the unhappy existence you're living is proof of that. Bernie, think about it…You're here because you had a heart attack. And you did it to yourself. Need I say more?"

Suddenly, a look of despair appears on Bernie's face. In a flash, Bob disappears and reappears seated beside Bernie. He reaches out to touch Bernie's hand and says, "My friend, it's time to expose the bitter truth again."

Bernie clears his throat and makes an attempt to speak.

Bob raises his hand and quietly says, "It's time to listen. Do you think you can handle this?"

Bernie nods.

"We'll take this slowly. One step at a time."

"I'm listening, Bob."

"First of all, your natural state is that of joy and inner peace. Every single person on Earth is born in that state. I mean *everyone*. It's their responsibility and your responsibility to stay connected to that state. Just so you know, there are a great many people who do believe that happiness is choice, and when times are tough, even tragic, they make every attempt possible to make choices that will help them to stay connected to their natural state."

Bernie sits with his eyes closed and listens to what is being said.

66

◇◇◇

"Enjoyment kicks Motivation and Inspiration into High Gear. ALWAYS remember that! Write it down! Get it laminated and slap it on your refrigerator! Well...what are you waiting for? Write it down!"

– Bob

◇◇◇

You Put Your Happiness on Hold

"The reason you are having difficulty with this conversation is because on a very deep and personal level you know that you have not been happy for a majority of your adult life. You have never truly enjoyed the process of achieving your professional goals because you got caught up in one of the ego's most dangerous traps."

"What trap is that?"

"You put your happiness on hold," Bob says. "And you never realized you were doing it."

"What do you mean?" Bernie replies.

"Through the years, you have unconsciously created a mindset that signifies that you will not and cannot be happy until you reach a certain status in life. You actually believe that your happiness is dependent upon something that has to take place in the future."

Bob puffs out his chest and does a very impressive Bernie impression: "*'I'll be happy when I drive a nicer car than my brother in-law.' 'I'll be happy when I make more money.' 'I'll be happy when I achieve my goals.'* And on and on...that is absolutely insane, because happiness will always be a couple of steps ahead of you."

Bernie opens his eyes and looks at Bob. *"What he is saying is true,"* he thinks.

"The only time you can truly be happy is in the moment, because the moment is the only time in which your life takes place. Your life can't take place in the past and it can't take place in the future. But you have allowed the ego to deceive and convince you that you cannot enjoy your life until you achieve your professional goals. To make matters worse, you've carried that same mindset with you, along with a host of other toxic beliefs, to every other area of your personal life: Your tasks, daily chores, the everyday things that need to be done. Like picking up the dry cleaning, shopping for groceries and driving to the airport. Or pitching a new idea to a potential buyer. All of these things and more make up the process of your life. And more often than not, you've made no or very little effort at all to live in the moment and experience the process, let alone enjoy it. Would you like an example?"

Bernie hesitates, takes a deep breath and says, "Yes."

"I know you love your dog, Wally."

Suddenly, Bernie's entire attitude and body language changes. "You bet I do! He's always there for me. I tell him all my problems, and the best part is that he doesn't talk back. He simply sits and listens. Somehow, Bob, I swear he understands."

"Well, it has been said that I work in mysterious ways. There just may be a reason why the word Dog backwards spells *God*. Dogs are a good example of what unconditional love is all about."

Bernie smiles. "I've thought about that."

"As with so many other things in your life, you're not always living in the moment with Wally. I mean, you're there with him physically, but you're not allowing yourself to fully experience the process."

"What do you mean that I'm with him physically, but I'm not allowing myself to fully experience the process? What kind of spiritual or mental process is involved in taking care of a dog?"

"Like when you take Wally for a walk or bring him to the park to play fetch. Rather than participating in his playful ways and funny antics or observing the many benefits that walking and playing has to offer you, your mind begins to wander. You start thinking that you should be somewhere else or doing something else. Or you bring your toxic past experiences or your concerns about the future into the present moment. By doing that, you totally avoid the joy and laughter you could be experiencing in the moment. You'll never have that moment again."

As Bernie listens, he starts to think about all the times he has focused on upcoming meetings or failed opportunities instead of what he was doing in the moment. As he considers how he's been living his life in only the past and future, he starts to think that maybe he hasn't been living at all.

"Oh, and by the way," says Bob, "the next time Wally drops a ball in front of you, it may not be that he's trying to tell you that he wants to play. Maybe, just maybe, he's sensing that *you need* to play."

Bernie stares at the office wall as Bob continues to drop the truth like a great big bag of hammers.

"It all comes down to this: Bernie, you have to give yourself a break. You've gotta lighten up, kid. I know your life hasn't been easy, but you have a tendency to make things worse than they have to be. You focus a great part of your energy on what isn't working and what's lacking. You very rarely pat yourself on the back for a job well done, or acknowledge your accomplishments or your appreciation for all the good in your life. That's the stuff you have to focus on more often. Most of your life you've focused on all the negative stuff. And that stuff has become your reality. The sad part is that it isn't true –

but you believe that it's true, and that's all that matters in your world. The consequences have become quite severe."

Suddenly, Bernie realizes what he has been doing to himself, for most of his life, *from the inside out*. He lowers his head. A tear slowly drips down the side of his face.

"Don't be so hard on yourself, Bernie. You got caught up. You didn't realize that happiness can only be experienced in the present moment. You, like hundreds of millions of others, simply didn't know that you could choose to enjoy the process, let alone know how to do so, but all of that is going to change."

Bernie wipes his cheek and says, "So what's next, Bob?"

Bob claps and rubs his hands together energetically, as if he's going to dig into a big meal again. "Well...now that you know what's been keeping you from enjoying your life? What do you say we work on how to fix it?"

Bob notices that Bernie is still in a low mood.

"You're the boss, Bob," Bernie says quietly. "Whatever you say."

Smiling from ear to ear, Bob says, "Great choice of words Bernie! Great choice of words! I like that. *The Boss*...It has a certain ring to it. I just might use that instead of 'Bob.' What do you think, Bernie?"

Bernie looks up at Bob and chuckles. "You might have to take that up with Springsteen's lawyers!"

Bob laughs. "That a boy, Bernie! I knew you had it in you."

"Had *what* in me?"

"See how much better you feel now that you've allowed yourself to laugh? That was your choice. Just a moment ago your energy level plummeted, and with one little chuckle your attitude shifted. That's what laughter does, Bernie. Laughter charges your inner battery and helps you cope with tough times."

"Are you suggesting that I should laugh it up a little more?" says Bernie.

"A SHIFT from pain to laughter is a miraculous happening...Holy SHIFT!"

– Bob

"I'm not just suggesting," says Bob. *"I'm telling you* that you have to take time out of each day and laugh. Why do you think people go to comedy clubs, watch sitcoms or see funny movies? Because they want to laugh. Why do they want to laugh?"

Bernie tries not to laugh as he speaks. "For the same reason they want to have sex. It simply makes them feel good."

"Bingo!" says Bob, laughing. "Seriously, Bernie, a physiological, mental, emotional, and – might I say – spiritual reaction takes place when you allow yourself to laugh. Even if you are having a really bad day, when you laugh, life doesn't seem that bad after all."

B O B's

High Points to Remember

When you make a conscious choice to enjoy yourself during the process of achieving your goals, you become more creative, more productive, more resilient, and you find solutions to problems a lot quicker. That's a promise, my friend.

Passion and Enthusiasm are two forces that are key to creating the things you desire. The energy they radiate will not only increase your overall degree of attention, but also generate a powerful connection to me and my energy field. In fact, the word Enthusiasm comes from the Greek word 'entheos.' Meaning the God within. Or, in this case, the Bob within.

The only time you can truly be happy is in the moment, because the moment is the only time in which your life takes place. Your life can't take place in the past and it can't take place in the future.

8

Become a Humor Being

> "Laughter is the pit-stop in the rat race of life. In that it gives you enough emotional fuel and repairs to get back in the race again."
>
> – STEVE RIZZO (I'M JUST SAYING!)

ernie reflects on what Bob just said. "I get your point, Bob. Laughter is a very important life strategy."

"In more ways than you think," says Bob.

"What do you mean?" asks Bernie.

"A sense of humor is more than just one's ability to laugh. Laughter is a by-product of humor, a very important by-product, but still just a part of the many wonderful healing qualities that a sense of humor has to offer."

"How so?"

Bob reaches over his shoulder, grabs a dictionary from the shelf and places it on the desk in front of Bernie. "Your dictionary says the word *sense* means perception or awareness; and correct reasoning; or sound judgment. The word *humor* is the mental quality that produces absurd or joyful ideas. So, we can say that a sense of humor is to have perception or to be aware that you have a mental quality to turn your mind or mood to produce joyful or absurd ideas that can soothe your soul. The initiative and proficiency by which you utilize your 'sense of humor,' however, comes from what I call your *Humor Being*."

"Humor Being…" says Bernie. "I love the way that sounds."

Bob smiles. "As you should, my friend. Everyone on Earth is born with their own internal Humor Being. Unfortunately, most people, for whatever reason, live their entire lives without ever knowing they have this powerful gift within them, let alone how to tap into and make it work for them. Your Humor Being is part of your Higher Nature. It's the part of you that brings out the best of who you are when times get tough. What your Humor Being gives you more than anything else is emotional stability and peace of mind."

"So, making a habit of invoking my HB will help turn me into a happier person with a brighter outlook?"

"Bernie, tapping into your HB, as you put it, is a strategy that can help you cope with the natural ups and downs of life. Instead of allowing unfortunate situations, unlucky circumstances and foul people to suck the energy right out of you, you can turn to your HB for a levity break. Those who make the shift and live in harmony with their Humor Being have the ability to see the bright side of a negative situation. They embrace change more easily and make conscious choices to enjoy themselves during the process of whatever they are trying to achieve. As we discussed earlier, your natural state is that of joy and inner peace. It's your responsibility to stay connected to that state each and every day, and the main job of your Humor Being is to help you maintain that connection. After all, humor is one of the qualities that makes you human, so why not use it?"

> *"Sometimes all you need is a few seconds to catch your second wind. Laughter…your Humor Being gives you that few seconds time and time again."*
>
> *– Bob*

Bernie looks at Bob and says, "It is amazing the power we derive from simply stepping outside our emotions of the moment, giving ourselves permission to make a shift and viewing them from a humorous perspective."

"It sure is. And you don't have to be a comedian armed with an arsenal of rapid-fire funny remarks or wisecracks to give your Humor Being the opportunity to express itself. What's important is not necessarily to *be* funny, but rather to allow yourself to *see* the funny in a stressful or challenging situation. This is a habit anyone can master. The more you challenge yourself to see the humor during adverse times, the more your Humor Being will become a part of who you are. The more your HB becomes a part of who you are, the more you will be able to enjoy your life."

"So, when should I tap into my HB?" Bernie asks.

Bob stands up from his desk and begins pacing the room. Bernie's eyes follow him with every step.

"Every day!" says Bob. "But especially when you become aware that your emotions are veering out of control."

"How do you determine they're heading in that direction?"

"Stop, take a deep breath and ask yourself any number of the following warning questions." As Bob continues speaking, the chalk once again levitates and begins writing on the board:

What will be the consequences if I hold on to this anger?

I have an important meeting with a client. Am I putting my best foot forward now?

What will happen if I don't get my shift together?

I have an extremely busy day. Am I in the mood I need to be in to get things done?

Are my fears keeping me from succeeding?

What can I do to turn this mood around?

What would Bob say if he could see me now?

"These types of questions act like radar, warning you that you're spinning out of control and becoming dangerously negative. More importantly, warning questions are good reminders that there are better ways to deal with frustrating and chaotic events than clinging to the worst-case scenarios they bring up. Here is one humorous strategy to get you on your way. The next time you're at the breaking point of losing it, imagine that your Humor Being has a voice and is taking on the role of a news commentator giving you the blow-by-blow account of what is happening inside you."

Bob lowers his voice, and he sounds strangely like Morgan Freeman...

"We interrupt your regularly scheduled life to bring you this special news bulletin! This is a message from your emotional broadcasting system. It has been brought to our attention that you are late and stuck in traffic, and that your back sweat is turning your seat into the Everglades! You are now being tested to evaluate the severity of the negative situation. Right now, you have a choice! You can either get your shift together and laugh, learn the lesson life is trying to teach you, nourish your soul, move on with confidence and enjoy the day, or you can suffer from inner conflict, get angry, lose control and let opportunities pass you by! May the shift be with you....back to you in the studio, Chuck."

Bernie looks confused and says, "Who's Chuck?"

"Never mind, Bernie," Bob says, shaking his head. *"Never mind."*

B⬤B's

High Points to Remember

Your Humor Being is of your Higher Nature. It's the part of you that brings out the best of who you are when times get tough. What your Humor Being gives you more than anything else is emotional stability and peace of mind."

Those who make the shift and live in harmony with their Humor Being have the ability to see the bright side of a negative situation. They embrace change more easily and make conscious choices to enjoy themselves during the process of whatever they are trying to achieve."

Seriously, a physiological, mental, emotional, and, might I say, spiritual reaction takes place when you allow yourself to laugh. Even if you are having a really bad day, when you laugh, life doesn't seem that bad after all."

Part 3

"An attitude of gratitude simply makes you feel good. A state of feeling good is a sure sign that you are connected to my energy field."

– Bob

When SHIFT happens, your life changes. Bob shows Bernie how to shift his way of thinking to create greater joy and enthusiasm and new levels of success. Bob also reminds Bernie that as long as he keeps thinking in limiting ways he will never be able to experience opportunities that are on the horizon.

9

Get Your SHIFT Together

> "When I started counting my blessings, my whole life turned around."
>
> — WILLIE NELSON

ob sets the hourglass back down and turns abruptly. "Bernie, right now I want you to stand up."

Bernie stands and faces the chalkboard.

"Repeat after me," says Bob.

Bernie listens as he watches the chalk write *"I am the creator of my success and happiness."*

"I am the only problem I will ever have, and somewhere within me is a solution waiting to be discovered."

"I get what I think about, whether I want it in my life or not."

"Life is a process, and the process is my life."

"And I will make every attempt to enjoy my life."

"Even if I don't know how," Bernie mumbles.

Bob stands behind Bernie and places his hands firmly on top of Bernie's shoulders. "Well, my friend!" Bob says energetically, "I'm going to show you how. As I said earlier, this isn't brain surgery. It's brain adjustment that will help you create the life you desire, my man! What we are going to do is to implement a regular routine so you will not only enjoy the journey towards your professional and personal goals, but also the process of life in general. I'm going to show you how to create some basic habits so you can become a happier you!"

"Really?" Bernie asks. "I've just spent about twenty minutes reliving moments in which I've failed to do just that. I'm not sure I'm capable."

Even as Bernie is frowning, Bob is grinning like a lunatic. "Yes, really!" he shouts. "Bernie, before we go any further, as I stated earlier, it's important that you keep an open mind about what you're going to hear. These strategies may appear to be simplistic at face value, but don't doubt their significance. Trust me when I say that if you allow them to become a part of who you are, you will simultaneously be connecting to who I am. Then you will notice a dramatic difference in how you view life and how life treats you. These strategies will always bring out the best in you when times get tough. And that, my friend, is part of what miracles are all about. Got it?"

"Got it, Bob. You have my word. My mind is open and clear."

Reprogram Your Subconscious

"Great! The purpose here is to help you create a healthy mindset so that no matter how tough your circumstances are you will be able to shift your focus to what's working rather than fixate on what isn't. The best way to do this is to reprogram your subconscious mind."

"My subconscious mind?"

"Your subconscious mind runs 90 to 95 percent of your life and doesn't know the difference between true or false. It only knows the information you program into it. Up until this point you have created a belief system that signifies lack of enjoyment, chaos and victimization. That, primarily, is why your life isn't working. What I mean is that your subconscious has been taken over by the ego and the forces of negativity. So, we need to reprogram your subconscious with habits that will give you the attitude and motivation needed for you to live a successful, happier life. Is this making sense to you?"

"So far so good, Boss Bob." Bernie smirks. "But I can't vouch for how my subconscious is taking it all in."

"Good. It seems to be working already. Now this whole process of reprogramming your subconscious starts every night before you go to sleep."

Bernie exhales heavily. "Well, Bob, we have a problem there. I usually have a tough time sleeping."

"I know," says Bob. "Wouldn't you agree that in order to have a good night's sleep, you have to feel good about yourself?"

"That makes sense to me."

"Therein lies the problem. How in the world can you feel good if you keep focusing on all the stuff that makes you anxious, frustrated and angry? So...every night, as you're getting ready to go to bed, I want you to spend a few minutes thinking of all of the things you are grateful for during that day. This is especially important when you've had a bad day and it seems as though there is nothing to give thanks for."

"Wow! Talk about challenges!" says Bernie.

"I understand that sometimes finding something to be grateful for can take work, especially when negative emotions are getting the best of you, but this is important. You have to understand that gratitude is a discipline, and it involves a conscious choice. Thoughts of gratitude eventually create an attitude of gratitude. Bernie, you can choose to be grateful even when your emotions are still steeped in hurt and resentment. Sometimes you just have to push yourself."

"An Attitude of Gratitude is a discipline that's worth acquiring. It creates an immensely powerful connection to ME."

– Bob

Bernie thinks for a moment and says, "It's a matter shifting my way of thinking."

"Exactly!" says Bob. "Maybe you closed a deal with a business associate or had a few laughs with a friend. Maybe you received a compliment. Or maybe you did something nice for someone and it lifted your spirits. It can be something as small as a snack you had or a parking space you snagged. Believe me, you'll come to find that it's well worth the effort. Because you will be creating an attitude of gratitude, which is a habit that's conducive to success and enjoying your life."

"I get it, Bob. I mean, I can understand how being grateful can make me feel better."

"Great!" says Bob. "Then, as soon as you get under the covers, I want you to relax and focus on your breathing. *Breathe in… breathe out. Inhale…exhale.*" Bob smiles as Bernie is breathing along with his instructions. "Very good, Bernie. Then, once you feel a sense of calm, take a few moments to program your subconscious by repeating affirmations that begin with 'I Am' and 'I deserve.'"

Bob pauses and looks at Bernie. "Are you getting all of this?"

"Yes," says Bernie. "I really am." Bernie notices the chalk gliding towards the blackboard. It starts writing as Bob continues to speak.

"For example, '*I am capable of handling any challenge that comes my way. I am smart enough to achieve my goals. I deserve to be successful. I deserve to be prosperous. I deserve to be happy.*'"

Bob looks over at Bernie and gives him a sly look. "And, of course, your favorite, Bernie. '*I deserve ten million dollars.*'"

Bernie screams out. "Yeah baby! That's what I'm talking about!"

Bob laughs. "I'm so glad I broke the mold when you were born."

"Are you saying I'm one of a kind?"

"Yes, thank *Me*. Let's continue. After you've finished with 'I am' and 'I deserve,' as you close your eyes to sleep, imagine what it would be like if you had all of the things you wanted in life. It's important that you imagine it as if you already had it. I want you to really get into this. Got it?"

"I got it," Bernie says. He closes his eyes and pretends to snore.

Bob smirks. "Very funny."

"I'm just practicing using my HB, Boss."

"Fine. Ready to learn the wake-up routine that works?"

"I am."

Starting Your Day with an Unstoppable Attitude

Bob continues: "As soon as you open your eyes to start the day, before you take the covers off and put your feet on the floor and put on your fuzzy slippers, know that the creation of your day has begun and, *more importantly*, know that *you* are the creator. Know that you can steer your thoughts and emotions in the direction you want them to go. Not in the direction they are so often telling you to go. In other words…you can choose to seize the day or you can let the day seize you."

"Or, I can choose to seize the alarm clock, throw it out the window and pull the covers over my head and go back to sleep."

"Ha!" Bob laughs. "Time will fly without your help, my friend! But if you *clocked* anyone walking by outside, they'd be in for a hard *time!*"

Bernie chuckles and groans. "Bob, you sure are full of Dad Jokes."

Bob smiles. "Remember, life is filled with choices, Bernie. My point is that too many people start their days in low moods. To make matters worse, they're not aware of what they're doing to themselves. It has become a part of their personality. This is because they start their day in a problem-solving state of mind. As soon as they wake, before they even take the covers off, they start thinking of the challenging, if not grueling, time they had the day before...the fires that weren't put out, the irate people they had to deal with and all of the things that need to be done today…and they aren't even out of bed yet. Then, they can't understand why they're always feeling anxious, overwhelmed and totally exhausted."

"You were just describing me, weren't you?" asks Bernie.

"You know what they say, if the fuzzy slipper fits…"

"And if the slipper does fit?" Bernie ducks as he hears the chalk buzz past his head towards the blackboard.

"If the shoe fits, then it's time to Get Your Shift Together!" says Bob. "*In other words, when you wake up in the morning, before you put one foot on the floor, rather than focusing on what isn't working and what needs to be done, I want you to shift your focus and way of thinking to what is working in your life…to something that gradually makes you feel good, that lifts your spirit, or something you truly appreciate or are grateful for.*"

The chalk scribbles this furiously.

"This takes an attitude of gratitude to a higher level doesn't it?" asks Bernie.

"Yes," says Bob. "And it really doesn't matter what or who it is. Maybe you're putting your attention on Wally lying at the foot of your bed or a particular friend who always makes you laugh. It could be a wonderful meal you had the night before or the breakfast you're going to have that morning. Maybe you're having friends over to watch the football game on Sunday. Whatever it is, it's important that you feel it with your heart and soul. Really get into this!"

Bernie is getting excited about this new possibility. Instead of toiling over what was and what could be, the secret is as easy as having fun in every moment! "What about my garden?" he asks. "I absolutely love my garden, Bob! I have a natural habitat in my back yard, complete with a variety of beautiful trees, flowers and wildlife. It's my escape from all of the chaos!"

"Absolutely!" says Bob. "You see, Bernie, your only goal is to make sure you feel good, confident and energized to meet the day."

"That's always my choice and responsibility. Right, Bob?"

"Right, Bernie! An attitude of gratitude fills your heart with joyful, high-energy feelings of being blessed with the many things you already have, rather than fixating on what you don't have – or what's not working."

"What a great way to start the day!"

"It sure is! And it only takes a few moments to create this attitude. It takes longer for me to explain it than it does for you to do it. Bernie, an attitude of gratitude is one of the most powerful connections you have to your Higher Self. You always want to start your day connected to your better angels because it assures your connection to me. The stronger that connection is, the better you will feel. The better you feel, the more creative and productive you are."

"And the more creative and productive I am, the better I feel." Bernie pauses, as if amazed at what he's just learned. "Wow! This wonderful, mysterious cycle continues as the manifestation process works in my favor."

Bob nods dramatically. "That's right, my friend. It's the best kind of snowball effect. It places you in a solution-discovery state of mind. Which, in turn, helps you to view your challenges as an adventure."

"Which, in turn, makes life more exciting!" says Bernie.

"Exactly!" says Bob. "Fully appreciating where you are and loving what you have in the moment are key to getting what you want. So, don't be surprised when good things start coming into your life."

"I guess having an attitude of gratitude is a great part of the Universal Magnet that attracts the things I desire most."

"Absolutely!" says Bob. "Thoughts of Gratitude throughout the day take you out of your fear state and keep you from entering into the Negative Zone. It's an emotional sign that something good just happened to you or that something favorable is happening to you." Bob notices that Bernie isn't quite grasping everything. "Speak what's on your mind, Bernie.

Bernie gives a slight chuckle. "Can you elaborate a little more about how and why gratitude is an emotional sign that something good is happening to me?"

"Certainly," says Bob. "Remember what I said about your subconscious running 90 to 95 percent of your life?"

"Yes," says Bernie. "That it doesn't know the difference between true or false. It only knows the information I program into it."

"Right," says Bob. "To put it another way, your subconscious is so objective that it doesn't know the difference between an experience in your life that creates an emotion and an emotion you can create by your thoughts alone. To your subconscious, it's exactly the same."

Bernie contemplates what Bob just said. "Okay...okay...so... when I begin to feel gratitude, my subconscious is actually believing that something favorable is going to happen to me, or already has happened to me."

"Yes. And the emotional characteristics of gratitude are the perfect characteristics of the state of energy for you to receive. In other words, my friend, when you consistently envision and embrace your future and feel gratitude for it, you will believe that the future is more of a reality because it's equal to the emotion you're experiencing."

Bernie contemplates. "But...I'm feeling the emotion before the actual event occurs...or the actual desire is fulfilled...right?"

"Right, you are." Bob allows Bernie more time to figure it out.

"So...In a sense, I use gratitude as a strategy to elevate my energy...and when I do, throughout the day, every day, I am on my way to manifest the things I desire and to create a brighter future... all I can say is WOW!"

"I love the way you're thinking, Bernie. An attitude of gratitude simply makes you feel good. Feeling good is the fuel that drives motivation and inspiration. Being truly motivated and feeling inspired are sure signs that you are connected to my energy field. It's started already."

> *"Don't clutter your brain thinking about everything that needs to be done; rather, think about who you have to be in order to get it done."*
>
> *– Bob*

Bernie looks over at the hourglass, watching the sands trickle steadily through. "I should have been thinking like this a long time ago."

"*Would-a, should-a, could-a,*" says Bob. "What you did in the past is over and absolutely irrelevant to what you can do from this point on. Live in the moment, Bernie."

"You're right, Bob."

"Here's my promise to you. Commit to making an attitude of gratitude a part of your waking-up process. This will engage your subconscious to create a pathway to make enjoying the process a new habit and creating the life you want. Think of it as breakfast for your soul."

"Nice! Cosmic bacon and eggs! Then, goodbye challenges and problems."

"No, not at all," says Bob. "Bernie, I'm not claiming you won't be confronted by challenges. Of course, you will, whether or not you've soothed your soul with universal oatmeal. There will always be obstacles of some kind to overcome. There will be times when chaos and negative forces surround you, but you don't have to let them inside. It may not be easy at first, but as you condition yourself to prepare for the day ahead with gratitude, joyful statements and positive visualization, you will notice that stressful outside forces don't bother you as much. Ultimately, what you're doing is creating the ability to bounce back, and that's an important life skill – one you need to master. It comes down to this: the unexpected is waiting for you. Countless outside factors can make or ruin your day, many of which are not in your direct control."

Bernie thinks about this. "So, it just makes sense to seize control of what I can?"

"Absolutely. No matter whether you're in an up or down period, always remind yourself that true happiness and inner peace is your number one priority."

"Focusing on what makes me grateful and what's working in my life puts me on the path to happiness and the ability to enjoy the day, which, in turn, will make my connection to you more powerful."

Bob leans back. He looks immensely pleased. "That is exactly why you have to make the shift to start your day in a good mood and maintain your feelings of appreciation throughout the day. Even one situation a day in which you are able to invoke your grateful feelings and choose to be happy in the moment can have a tremendous impact on your life. You're a baseball fan, right?"

"You know it! The Bronx Bombers! My coffin lining will be pinstripes!"

"Well, then you know that the difference between an all-star major league career and spending a frustrating tour of dusty towns in the minor leagues is about one hit a week. One measly hit a week over the course of a season can make such a difference. That is what I'm talking about when I say waking up with a good attitude will create success. It's incremental. I don't mean to suggest that you will become Babe Ruth, but it's important to remember that he struck out far more often than he hit home runs."

"Well," says Bernie. "If I do become the next Babe Ruth, I'll be sure to wave my cap to the crowd after every home run as I'm eating a hot dog."

B⛰B's

High Points to Remember

When you wake up in the morning, before you put your foot on the floor, rather than focusing on what isn't working and what needs to be done, I want you to shift your focus and way of thinking to what is working in your life…to something that gradually makes you feel good, that lifts your spirit, or something you truly appreciate or that you're totally grateful for."

An attitude of gratitude is a discipline that simply makes you feel good. Feeling good is the fuel that drives motivation and inspiration. Being truly motivated and feeling inspired are sure signs that you are connected to my energy field."

There will be times when chaos and negative forces surround you, but you don't have to let them inside. It may not be easy at first, but as you condition yourself to prepare for the day ahead with gratitude, joyful statements, and positive visualization, you will notice that stressful outside forces don't bother you as much."

10

The Wrath of Negativity

"No one can create negativity or stress within you. Only you can do that by virtue of how you process your world."

– WAYNE DYER

*T*he fire continues to throw Bernie's shadow onto the far wall. He tries not to be distracted by the magic chalk, which is now doodling a motorcycle in the corner of the chalkboard. "So, if I imagine what I desire with a strong degree of attention, think positive thoughts, visualize, make every attempt to enjoy the process and take action with passion and enthusiasm, the law will work for me, not against me?" he asks.

"Actually," says Bob, "the Law has to work *with* you. This is important to know. The absolute truth is that you never create by yourself. The ego fools people into believing *they* are manifesting their own desires. That's where free will got misinterpreted. In fact, whether people know it or not, it is always a co-creation with me, the energy field, the Source, the universe, or whatever you choose to call my involvement. Your job is to go beyond the voice of your ego and allow connection to me and my energy field to bring you what you desire. This is a collaboration, and I can't -*laborate* without the *co-*, you dig?"

"Let go and let Bob, eh?" Bernie responds.

Bob laughs. "I can see the bumper sticker already. Yes. I already know what you want before you ask. You just have to learn to reconnect to my energy field, which is all around you – heck, you generate it – and plug into its vast creative powers."

"So, in a way, we're a team," Bernie says.

"In a way? In *all* ways and *always!* You are my creation. We are more than a team. You are a part of me and I am a part of you. Think of yourself as a very tiny portion of what makes me me."

Bernie lets it sink in for a moment. *I'm a part of the system – the grand plan. I'm a part of Bob…the universe.* He smiles.

"Bernie, your thoughts, emotions, beliefs, intention, attitude, and prayers during every moment of your life define your relationship with my energy field. And here's the clincher. All the circumstances in your life are my response to the way you have communicated with me and my energy field."

Bernie's face grows even redder than before.

"In other words, my friend, you can't pray for peace of mind and then get in your car and shout, *'Watch it, asshole!'* at everyone in traffic. You're not even aware that you take that anger and a host of other negative emotions with you throughout the day. Believe me when I say they have a major effect on every decision you make."

Bernie looks at the ground, shuffles his feet and nods in agreement.

"And another thing. It's also impossible to pray for success and then believe it won't happen just because the going gets tough. Where's the faith? How do you expect the things you desire to manifest when those transmissions are cancelling each other out?"

"Every time you think, feel or choose to act in a negative way, you run the risk of separating yourself from your natural state of joy and inner peace."

– Bob

Bob pauses to let this sink in.

"If you have doubt while you're praying, or if you walk away believing your prayers won't be answered, then what do you expect? Like attracts like. It's the Law of Cause and Effect. It's the Power of

Intention and the Law of Attraction in motion. The more you focus on your lack, the more lack you get back. The more you focus on what isn't working, the more your life won't work. The more..."

"Okay, okay!" Bernie shouts, raising his hands to the ceiling. "I get your point!"

"I hope you do. But just in case, I want to show you something." He claps his hands. The lights go out.

The lights abruptly return, and with them Bernie hears the familiar drone of airplane engines from inside the fuselage.

He looks around. Suddenly, he is on an American Airlines flight. He can tell by the flight attendants' uniforms and because his legs are cramped from the usual lack of leg room.

He turns to his right and has a sudden flash of déjà vu. The rosy-cheeked man next to him has already claimed all the elbow room and is leaning in to speak to him.

"A little tight in here, isn't it?" the man says with a smile.

Bernie ignores the man's comment, pulls out his iPhone and pretends to be looking at his messages.

"Are you here on business?" the man asks.

Still pretending to view his messages, Bernie can feel his body getting tense. "Yes, I'm here on business," he says. *Please make him shut up! Please!*

"What is it that you do?" the man cheerfully asks.

This pushed Bernie's buttons like nothing else. *People on planes, they have no respect for personal space. There's no etiquette anymore. I'm tired. I'm hungry. And the last thing I want to do is talk to this idiot about his middle management and his kids.*

> *"Does this type of inner dialogue sound familiar, dear reader?"*
>
> —*Bob*

Suddenly, Bernie realizes his train of thought has jumped back onto familiar rails. He thinks about what Bob said about praying for success and not being aware of the negative energy he is sending out.

Bernie turns to the man and is about to politely engage him in conversation, but to his complete horror, the words he hears himself speaking are not what he intended.

"Look, buddy," he says instead, "I've had a rough day, and I'd appreciate a little space in every way you can imagine." The words are coming out of his mouth, but Bernie has no control over them. He panics, but suddenly realizes why everything seems so familiar to him. He had taken this flight, and said those exact words, six years ago when he returned from a disappointing meeting in Salt Lake City. He was reliving the moment as if was happening in real time.

Bernie shifts his body to avoid any form of physical contact with his seatmate.

After a several minutes, the man turns again to Bernie and says, "You know, I couldn't help but overhear when you were on the phone earlier that you're in the solar energy business, and I'd like to ask you some...."

Bernie is mortified to hear the words coming out of his own mouth. "Tell you what. I can send you to a site where you can learn all about it. It's called Wikipedia. Or Google." Then, Bernie turns away and buries his head against the Naugahyde tombstone that the airlines try to pass off as a headrest.

"What am I doing?" he thinks. *"That guy was being perfectly nice, if not terribly thoughtful. And was that a GE logo ski jacket he was wearing? Holy crap, he could have been the seed possibility that Bob was talking about. Was he the answer to my prayers? Did I blow a perfect opportunity? I must have been out of my mind after that meeting!"*

Trapped in the prison of his own body, Bernie thinks back to that meeting more than five years prior. Things had not gone well. They hadn't gone terribly, but all the work Bernie had put into the presentation had been thrown out the window when the customer's AV link had gone out. Bernie had been forced to make the presentation without visuals, and it hadn't gone according to plan. He'd naturally been in a very bad mood when he boarded the plane.

Bernie hears a loud clap and is momentarily afraid that an engine has gone out. He blinks and finds himself instead briefly blinded in front of the desk lamp in Bob's office.

Chances and Choices

Bob speaks, ignoring Bernie's obvious disorientation. "So, you see, Bernie, sometimes the things you ask for come as seed possibilities and…"

"Wait a minute!" says Bernie. He shakes his head. "Wow! That was a total head trip!" His mind is reeling from what just transpired. "Wait just a minute!"

"No," Bob says. "I know what you're thinking Bernie, and you can forget it."

"Oh really? You're just going to shame me again? You turned the…whatever that was…off without showing me what could have happened? How would it have played out if I wasn't rude? What would have happened if I talked to the guy and he loved my idea? Did he give me the money to back it? Did he become my partner? Or did he introduce me to someone else who would have made my dream come true? I see where you're going, but you can't tease me without showing me what the potential was!"

Bob shrugs. "Yes, I do know what could have happened. No, I don't have to tell you. And I'm not going to."

"What?" Bernie says. "But why?"

"Because you're not supposed to know," Bob says. "That's all you need to know."

"So, I don't get to see what would have happened if I opened myself to the possibility of that moment on the plane?"

"No, but you can imagine what might have happened. I'm just giving you one of countless examples in which the system was working as intended, answering your transmissions and giving you an opportunity for manifestation."

Bernie looks thoughtful. "Not a lot of closure there, Bob, I gotta tell you. But I get it. I guess I was just wanting a little hope. Maybe a spark to show me I wasn't that far off after all."

Bob stands up, touches his toes and arches his back, extending his hands towards the ceiling of the office. "Tell ya what," he says. "Being eternity old really does a number on your back." He walks around the desk and sits in the chair next to Bernie. "Remember *Choose Your Own Adventure* books?"

"Yeah," says Bernie. "My son used to bring those home from the school library. You'd pick an option, flip to the page, and when you fall in a pit or some other challenging situation, you flip back to wherever you last were and try again. There were endless combinations of choices and stories."

"Exactly," Bob says. "How boring would it be if you made it through the book knowing all the right choices already? Your adventure into the unknown is where you experience who you are and what you're made of. It's where your character is being tested and molded. When you take that leap of faith you are sending a message to yourself as well as the entire universe that you are not only here, but qualified and ready to face any challenge along the way. You may be on top one day and suddenly fall the next, but think about this – isn't it better to fall than not to try at all?"

"Achievement does not make the person. The goal is just a gift. It's how you've lived and what you've done to achieve the goal that brings value to it."

– Bob

"I get that," says Bernie. "But all I've ever been taught is to plan and execute, to take the right steps in the right order, to be strategic about life. Avoiding risk is the name of the game. I took risks, and I felt punished for taking them!"

Bob puts a hand on Bernie's shoulder. "Bernie, you can strategically plan your personal and professional life, you can make careful choices and take what you think are the appropriate actions to fulfill the ideal life you want. But there is absolutely no way of knowing with certainty what will happen. Life is a risk itself. There are just too many variables and unexpected twists and turns that come into play. Even when your prayers are answered there are no sure ways of knowing how your life will turn out in the long run. Well, guess what, Bernie? You're not supposed to. If you did, the thrill of life would cease to exist."

"What do you mean?" asks Bernie. "Even if by some miracle I manage to balance my risk-averse nature *and* my prayers are answered that there is no sure way of knowing how my life will wind up in the long run?"

"You've heard the saying," says Bob. "Be careful what you pray for, because it might be answered."

"Heard it all my life," says Bernie.

"Well, let's say that your prayer for an angel investor in your solar energy endeavor was answered, and that your conversation with the gentlemen on the plane led to great success, and you became very wealthy as a result."

"Yeah, baby! That's what I'm talking about!"

Bob releases Bernie's shoulder and waves his hands when he speaks. "Get a grip, Bernie! This is hypothetical, remember. And I'm not finished."

Bernie looks contrite. "Sorry, Bob. Please continue."

"What if, because your prayer was answered, a whole new set of plans and circumstances came into play? As a result, your lifestyle changed drastically, and one of those changes meant you had to travel extensively."

"So what? With all my new wealth I could fly first class and not worry about elbow room wars with some mouth-breather, or even buy my own jet!"

"My point is that you have no idea. You also could have been killed in a plane crash on your way to a business meeting as a result of your newfound success. Or you could have met the woman of your dreams and lost her years later due to an illness. Or you could have lost your wealth in one year because your business tanked. I could go on and on. The scenarios and possibilities as a result of the choices you make along the way are endless and mind-boggling. This is why I cannot tell you what would have happened if you had behaved like a decent person on that plane."

Bernie shrugs. "The Bob giveth, and the Bob taketh away, right?"

Bob finally frowns, gets up and stares into a fireplace that he creates out of thin air.

"Bernie," he says, "I assure you, if either one of those scenarios had taken place, I would have had nothing to do with it. They would have been the result of the choices *you* made. You are way more in control of your life than you think."

Bernie stands up and walks beside Bob to look into the flames. "But I also could have lived happily ever after, right? I mean everything could have worked out in my favor?"

"Absolutely," Bob says.

"I guess anything can happen in the game of life," say Bernie.

"Actually," Bob says, "a John Lennon lyric said it best. *'Life is what happens while you're busy making other plans.'*"

"Yeah, and look what happened to him eventually."

"My point exactly!" says Bob, pointing at a curling flame in the fireplace. "The unexpected happened to him. After years of inner turmoil and isolation from fame, fortune and the music business, John Lennon got his life together and then came out of seclusion. He was making a huge comeback when he was suddenly killed by a crazed fan."

"I was deeply saddened by that. I mean, it really affected me."

"I know it did. It was a huge loss for millions all over the planet. But, Bernie, here is the beginning of the answer to your question. What if John Lennon somehow knew his fate was etched in stone; what if he knew he was going to be shot and killed by a crazed fan? Would he have come out of seclusion and into the limelight again? Or would he have stopped dancing to the song in his heart and suppressed his creativity along with the very essence of who he was?"

Bernie nods. "I see what you're getting at, but it's a tough stretch to compare my life to John Lennon's."

Bob walks back to take a seat. Bernie follows him. "Let's take this a step further. What if Abraham Lincoln, Martin Luther King Jr. or Gandhi knew their lives would be taken by an assassin's bullet simply because of who they were and what they believed? Would they have made different choices? Their accomplishments affected the lives of millions and, in some cases, billions of people. So, you see, this is why you shouldn't know the way it all ends and the way it all will go. I see how you may think you don't make much of a difference, but none of these people would have been influential at all if they hadn't carefully made one choice at a time and transmitted the right frequencies along the way."

"Right," Bernie says. "Our lives are better left to chance."

"*It's not just chance*," says Bob. "What's more important is *The Now*. The only time that matters is now – in the present moment. The present is the only place where you can live and learn. The present is where you can make a difference. The present is where you can truly express yourself and experience your natural state of joy. Five-year plans and financial planners and Miss Cleo can take a hike."

Bernie laughs.

"Here's another throwback," Bob says. "Awhile back, you were watching a Super Bowl at a hotel bar. There were well over 100 people in the lounge area. Everyone was yelling and cheering for their team to win."

"Yeah, Pats-Panthers! I remember it like it was yesterday! It was an incredibly close game. Every time one team scored or made a great play, fans would jump out of their seats and cheer their side on. The place was electric!"

Bob continues. "Indeed, they were, but who can deny that the enjoyment and the excitement was coming from the anticipation of not knowing which team was going to be victorious? My question to you is this: what would be the point in watching the Super Bowl or any other sporting event if you knew beforehand which team would win? Who can deny that it's in the not-knowing that makes it exciting? It's the same with the game of life, yours and everyone's on the planet. Unlike any other game, however, the goal is not just to win or to be the best, but rather to follow your heart regardless of your circumstances."

"Yeah, I see that. My Dad always used to refer to it as the 'school of life' as well."

Bob strikes the iconic Heisman trophy pose. "Whether you view life as a dance, a school, a game or a test doesn't matter. The key to a happy, successful life is not in knowing what the future holds in store for you. You must participate in the moment. *Every* moment. The fortunate among you know this in a profound way. And they live accordingly. They participate knowing there's a chance they can fall and lose it all. They're willing to play the Game of Life aware that defeat is a possibility, but they choose to focus on a victorious outcome. They're anxious to attend the School of Life knowing they will be subjected to difficulties, challenges, loss and tragedy, but as long as they learn the lessons, they will prevail. In short, they know there are no guarantees…only choices. The right to choose one's own way. And that choice happens every second of every day."

Nourish the Seeds of Possibility

"I realize I'll never know what favor or misfortune life has in store for me, and I guess you're right. I'm not supposed to know. But thanks for making one thing very clear: I will never know what I'm made of if I don't participate in every moment of my life. Perhaps that's what I should pray for, the courage to take a chance…to participate in the moment with the right way of thinking and an optimistic attitude."

Bob's brilliant smile fills the room. "That would be a wise choice. And speaking of prayer, let's get back to the plane ride."

Bernie tenses as he thinks about how he shrugged off what now seems like an answer to his prayers.

Bob doesn't notice or care as he wanders around his office examining items. He stops at a window that was not there before and picks up a small pot of soil. "As I said earlier, sometimes answers to prayers come as seed possibilities that in time will grow into the desire you want to manifest. The seed, however, will not grow without the proper care and nourishment it needs in order for it to take root and blossom into its full potential. That's your job."

As Bob speaks, a small, green shoot of plant life emerges from the pot, striving upward as if filmed in stop-motion.

"So, if that guy on the plane was a seed possibility, my negative attitude stopped the seed from taking root?" Bernie says.

With a wave of his hand, Bob coaxes the potted plant to grow. "Yes."

"And that's what you mean when you say I have to meet you halfway. In that particular instance, my job was to nourish the seed to allow the prayer to take root."

"Bingo," says Bob, opening his right hand just as the orchid blossoms.

"I guess you can say you're the creator and planter of the seed, and I'm the gardener?"

Bob again seems excited, but gingerly places the pot again on the windowsill before pumping his fist in the air. "Yes! Yes, that's right! Way to go, Bernie! Before and during prayer, or if you are creating a business plan, or writing out your goals, or really anything at all that needs to be accomplished during the day, it is up to you to first cultivate your state of consciousness, which is your garden, with positive thoughts, words and the right attitude so the seed can take root."

"Then, once the seed is planted, it's essential for me to continue to nourish the seed possibility with a steady flow of nutrients from the streams of faith, the right attitude and a constructive way of thinking. That's how I stay connected to your energy field."

Bob takes an abrupt step back and speaks. "Wow! You are really impressing me here. Just remember, Bernie, seed possibilities to prayers can come in many guises. Such as in the form of a book, an inspiring movie, lyrics to a song, an advertisement, a dream, an idea that hits you as you're exercising, walking your dog, driving your car, shopping or taking a shower. You have to be open to it in any moment, not just when you've decided it's appropriate."

Bernie thinks about Bob's flight re-creation. "Or, as I've just witnessed, in a conversation with a total stranger."

"Right. Acknowledging every moment as an opportunity to transmit and receive is your choice and your responsibility. I mean, sometimes opportunity is right in front of you screaming, 'Hey pal, I'm right here in front of you! Take advantage of me! This is what you asked for!'"

"I know I haven't been the most receptive, I guess," says Bernie. "But what is it that's blinding me from these opportunities? I feel like I've been playing by the rules I've been taught."

"Mmhmm. Rules," says Bob. "I'm glad you used the word *blinding*. It's impossible for anyone to acknowledge opportunity if they can't see it. And the reason they can't see it is because of their attitude. They lack faith. They're consumed with negative emotions. All negative emotions, Bernie, are destroyers of the spirit. They keep the light from your Higher Self – *which, as you know, is your connection to me* – from shining. If your light isn't shining when opportunity arises, if you're not in the right state of consciousness, opportunity lies dormant in the darkness. In a short period of time, it will simply fade away. Its purpose is lost. As my favorite Queen song goes, 'And another one bites the dust!'"

"You create your own hell when, for whatever reason, you don't make the SHIFT to view your challenges from a higher part of yourself."

– Bob

Bernie is beginning to feel warm. He thinks briefly that the fireplace must be radiating out towards him, but he looks at the wall and the fireplace has vanished again, replaced with wooden paneling. He thinks maybe it's the realization that he's in control of his own destiny that is warming him.

"So, I have to remember that every moment is an opportunity to invoke the Universal Law in making my connection to you, the Source, work!" he says.

Bob smiles and nods. "Yes. Your responsibility to yourself as well as to the universal law is to make sure you are inwardly poised and to keep your thoughts positive and loving – in spite of the injustice or chaos around you. That's what faith is all about."

"That's a huge responsibility." Bernie sighs. He wishes the fire was back.

"Yes, it is," says Bob. "I know what you've gone through. It takes an incredible amount of resiliency to give thanks to good things when you've lost so much, but here's a hard fact. You might have a perfect right to be angry at some injustice that has taken place in your life, but you also have a right to nervous disorders, migraines, digestive problems and the various manifestations of chaos that will consume you – and, as you have just seen, in the passing of opportunities and the miserable existence that will inevitably follow."

Bernie shifts in his seat. He looks at the orchid blooming on the windowsill. Scratching the back of his head, he looks back at the wall to find the roaring, cracking fire returned, casting his shadow on the opposite wall.

Bob wanders over to it and rubs his hands in front of the flames. "All you have to do is give up on controlling your life. Focus on fueling the right kinds of transmissions in every single moment," he says.

"That's all, huh?" Bernie cracks.

B🏔B's

High Points to Remember

*Y*our thoughts, emotions, beliefs, intention, attitude and prayers every moment of your life define your relationship with my energy field. And here's the clincher. All the circumstances in your life are my response to the way you have communicated with me and my energy field.

*I*f you have doubt while you're praying or if you walk away believing your prayers won't be answered, then what do you expect? Like attracts like. It's the way the system works. It's the Law of Cause and Effect. It's the Power of Intention and the Law of Attraction in motion.

*A*ll negative emotions are destroyers of the spirit. They keep the light from your Higher Self from shining. If you're not in the right state of consciousness, opportunity lies dormant in the darkness. In a short period of time, it will simply fade away. Its purpose is lost. As my favorite Queen song goes, 'And another one bites the dust!'

11

Abracadabra!

"If you realized how powerful your thoughts are you would never think a negative thought."

– PEACE PILGRIM

Bob moves to a corner cabinet and pours a glass of water for himself and one for Bernie.

"If you expect to prevail during tough times," he says, "you must understand that it is your current perception of the situation that either gives you hope or makes you want to give up to a lost cause. If you're always thinking about how you can't get a fair shake, you will always feel miserable. Ever heard the saying *'Misery loves company'*? Being miserable doesn't exactly attract good things, does it? If you want to change your life for the better, start by consciously changing what you think and what you say."

"What do you expect, though? I'm only human. I mean, you created me. You should know that I have limitations, and how you created me affects the way I operate."

Bob sips his water. "Therein lies the problem and the challenge not only for you, but for humanity."

"What do you mean?"

"You are not *only human*. The way you say *'only human'* is very limiting. You are my most precious creation. You have no idea of the potential that lies dormant within you. You can create great things. Remember that you are a part of me, and that I am a part of you. You have magical qualities within you."

"Magical qualities? You talk as if I'm some kind of wizard. In case you haven't noticed, I'm Bernie Merrit, not Harry Potter."

"In a way, you are a wizard, and within you lie an abundance of transformational tools that can be used at your command. The most important of which is your magic wand, of sorts."

"My wand? I have a magic wand?"

"In a manner of speaking, your mind is your wand, and the magical power you control with it are your thoughts. *Abracadabra!*"

Bernie puffs air out through his mouth, making an exasperated sound. "My thoughts? I know from what you said that they're powerful...but magical?"

"Yes. In fact, your thoughts can create miracles. That is, if you use your *wand* properly. If your thoughts are primarily focused on lack and what's not working, then you will create chaos and unwanted things. If your thoughts and are primarily focused on love, joy and faith, then you can create miraculous happenings."

"Okay, now wait a minute. We talked about miracles earlier. I know *you* can create miracles, but aren't you getting just a little carried away? There's no way I can create a miracle."

"Of course, you can. In fact, your main purpose on Earth is to create miracles. Well...actually, we create them together. Remember, a miracle can be nothing more than a shift in perception. Miracles start with a single thought...an idea."

Bernie picks up his water glass and stares into it. "Okay, you've lost me here."

"Bernie, what do Thomas Edison, Alexander Graham Bell and the Wright Brothers have in common?"

"They're all dead?"

Bob cocks an eyebrow. "Really, Bernie?"

"Okay, all three were inventors...who are deader than I am. Just sayin'."

Bob affects the voice of a game show host. "You are absolutely correct! Bernie, you are the Grand Prize Winner! Tell him what he's won, Johnny!"

"Sometimes you scare me, you know."

"Remember what I said about enjoying the moment? That doesn't just apply to those who think they are only human. Lighten up, Bernie!"

Suddenly, Bob throws his water glass into the air. With a small 'pop,' the glass and its contents transform into confetti, some of which drifts down into Bernie's own glass.

"Have fun in life!" Bob says.

"Okay. What does this have to do with the four dead guys?"

"Right…Well, there was a moment in time where the light bulb, the telephone and a flying machine were just seed possibilities…ideas in the minds of the inventors. And by the way, Bernie, such ideas are seed possibilities or sparks that ignite the manifestation process of miracles-to-be."

As Bob continues to speak, the chalk works overtime to sketch three thought bubbles with images of the inventions within them.

"But the more *intention* they gave to those thoughts and ideas, the more similar thoughts came into play. The more similar thoughts that came into play, the stronger was their vibration to the Law of Attraction and my energy field…and so on and so on. Eventually, those small, insignificant thoughts multiplied and evolved into powerful beliefs. Those beliefs ignited an emotional surge of confidence and positivity. Those powerful emotions eventually led to an unstoppable attitude to succeed. This entire process led to taking action, which played out into their experience, and the Universal Law delivered wonderful circumstances and conditions to work in their favor, and their desires began to manifest. Were they confronted with challenges and obstacles along the way? Absolutely! But they kept forging ahead."

> *"The bottom line is this: when you are in a Feel-Good State of Mind, you are in alignment with who you really are – your True Self – your connection to Me."*
>
> *– Bob*

An eraser flies in and removes the thought bubbles from around the images, leaving only sketches of a light bulb, telephone and airplane behind.

"Until one day, behold, on all three accounts a miracle has taken place," Bob says. "What once seemed impossible, even ridiculed and laughed at by the great majority, became a miraculous happening for all to witness and praise. And all three, like all other inventions, discoveries, works of art, business endeavors and dreams that come true, theirs started with an idea...one simple thought – a simple shift in perception. A seed possibility. That, my friend, is how miracles happen."

Bernie looks at the chalkboard for a moment. "I really don't know what to say. It's so simple. Thoughts are the first step for all things to be. If you believe it hard enough, it will become reality."

Bob grins, stands up and gives Bernie a big round of applause. "Bravo! Bravo! I love that! And it rhymes!"

Bernie stands, takes a few bows and does his best impression of Elvis. "Thank you! Thank you very much! You're beautiful! Thank you very much!"

Laughing, Bob plops back down into his chair. "Seriously, Bernie, my greatest gift to humankind is the power of thought. I don't mean just the ability to decide between a salad and a sandwich for lunch. I'm talking about the ability to change your environment with your mind! It is the foundation of free will. As I said earlier, thoughts and the emotions they elicit are pure energy that can take you to the highest of highs or the lowest of lows."

"If thoughts are so powerful, and we have so many of them," Bernie says, "why isn't it easier? Thoughts are a dime a dozen. I have friends who have plenty of thoughts, and they're not shy in sharing them on a constant basis. I wouldn't pay a dime for a hundred of them. How can I make my thoughts work for me?"

Your Beliefs Write the Story of Your Life

"Okay...this is important, Bernie. Your thoughts create your beliefs. The beliefs you have about anything and everything in your life – your job, religion, sex, politics, money, love, how you perceive yourself and all that you desire, what you have and don't have – are formulated over a period of time through a consistent way of thinking. It's like I just explained with our inventor buddies. The more attention and intention they gave to their thoughts, the more like-thoughts came into play, and eventually those thoughts evolved into a powerful, unshakable belief. You know the rest."

"Miracles," Bernie says, as if stating the obvious.

"That's right. But beware, Bernie. Your beliefs can also be destructive. This happens when you allow yourself to bring your toxic past experiences or your fear-based thoughts of the future into the present moment."

"Okay, hold on. I'm trying to figure out the difference between thoughts and beliefs."

"This should help. A miracle can only take place in the present moment. It can't take place in the past, and it can't take place in the future." Bob pauses and extends an upward-facing palm to make sure Bernie is following. "So, if you expect a miracle to take place, it must be unencumbered by past or future worries. This is where most people have a problem."

"How so?"

"Just a few moments ago you were thinking you were flat broke."

"How did you know…? Oh, sorry. Of course, you would know. Anyway, it's true. I am practically broke. I've almost emptied my retirement fund on my bright ideas that never worked, and I'm spending more than I earn. If I wanted a steak dinner tomorrow, I'd have to put it on layaway. I have alimony payments. I'm having difficulty paying bills. I'm…"

Bob raises his hand for Bernie to stop. "What you are saying may be your financial condition now, but your current financial condition will only change when you change your state of consciousness. Right now, you are bringing your toxic past experiences and worries along with your concerns about the future into the present moment. This emotional upheaval only weakens your connection to my energy field. Remember, the Universal Law is always working. By allowing yourself to affirm out loud 'I am broke' or 'I don't have enough money,' you are not only choosing to compound the condition in the present, but also into future. If that's what you choose to think, then the universe will respond, *'Well, if that is what you think, then that is what you will get.'*"

"It's the Law! Like attracts like!" Bernie says.

"You got it," says Bob. "The more you focus on what you don't have and can't get, the more you provide the universe with opportunities to bring you experiences that reflect those beliefs."

"So my thoughts become my beliefs, which become my life. Wow!"

"'Wow' is right. Whether positive or negative, your beliefs impact your emotions, how you feel and how you view and react to the day-to-day circumstances and events that make up your daily life. The more you hold to the stories created by negative beliefs, the more you validate the false reality they represent. This continuing cycle has a profound effect on your destiny, both personally and professionally."

"Nothing can distort the way you view your life and your surrounding world more than Toxic Beliefs. They have the power to paralyze you physically, mentally, emotionally, and spiritually."

– Bob

"So, whether positive or negative, my beliefs are the foundation of my life. My success and happiness are built upon them."

"Absolutely. Haven't you noticed that some people have been given every advantage in life and still manage to sabotage their success and destroy their chance at happiness? Then there are those who seem to have every obstacle imaginable thrown in front of them and yet they still move ahead, refusing to give up. They take these obstacles and somehow manage to make their lives work and enjoy the process as they go. Haven't you ever asked yourself why?"

"I know people in both camps. I just assumed they were lucky or unlucky."

"I knew you would say that. People make their own luck by the way they think. The people in the latter group, consciously or unconsciously, shift their thoughts to create an empowering belief system. They acknowledge that they're going through tough times, but they don't fixate on an illness getting worse, a lack of funding, a bad break, a faltering economy or a business deal going sour. They primarily keep their emotions intact and focus their attention on what they want to produce. The lucky breaks, the right people, the fortunate circumstances, successful opportunities and serendipitous events come their way as a result of their intense intention and contemplation. Everyone has the power to do this. It's something of a Jedi mind-shift. You have this ability, too."

"Really? First, I'm Harry Potter, now I'm Luke Skywalker?"

Bob points to a *Star Wars* poster that suddenly appears on the wall. *"May the Shift be with you."*

Bernie laughs.

"It's good to see you're getting your sense of humor back. By the way, *Star Wars* is a good example of the power of your thoughts."

"Oh yeah? How so?"

"First, I want you to understand what the phrase *'May the Force be with you'* is really all about. Do you remember who Obi-Wan Kenobi is?"

"Yes," Bernie says. "He was the mentor, right?"

Bob nods. "The Force is strong in this one. When Obi-Wan says *'May the Force be with you,'* he is actually saying let go of your human capabilities and let your Higher Self take over. The most profound scene in *Star Wars* is when Luke is in the middle of an intergalactic battle with the forces of evil, and he is losing control of his ship. Doubt and panic are starting to set in."

Bernie sees a connection. "Just like people lose control of themselves when negativity consumes them in the everyday battles of life?"

"Exactly! Great analogy! Then, out of nowhere, Luke hears the voice of Obi-Wan: *'Let go and let the Force take over, Luke.'* What he's really saying is, 'Let go of your limiting thoughts and let the true part of you, your Higher Self, or, in this case, *the Force*, take over. Right there, Luke's responsibility is to let go of all limiting human thoughts so he can let a more powerful entity take over."

"In other words," says Bernie, "when you've done all that's humanly possible, let go and let the very essence of you take over."

"Right answer again. Give the man any prize from the middle shelf," says Bob. "Let me take the wheel. But remember, in all matters of your life you have to let go of all limiting thoughts and beliefs in order to let me do my thing."

"Got it. So, the best way that people can make a strong connection to their Higher Self or to you and your energy is through the way they think?"

"Ultimately, yes. Daily small thoughts build into beliefs that become emotionally charged, high-bandwidth channels to my energy field. A little later on I will show you how to shift your way of thinking to make that connection to your Higher Self."

"Can you explain to me in more detail what you mean by my thoughts having magical powers?"

"Sure. Locked within the mind of every person are the answers to every problem and the secrets to all the mysteries they will ever face. Now, in ancient Sanskrit the word *man* literally means to 'think.'"

"I remember that from a philosophy course I took! The philosopher Descartes, right? *'I think, therefore I am?'*"

"Sort of," says Bob. "Descartes had it half right. But it goes beyond simply existing. It means you aren't just here, a person, because you think, but that you're a force that can affect the world around you by *what* you think."

"And that could be a good thing or a bad thing."

"You got that right. The great poet Milton said, *'The mind is its own place, and it can make a heaven of hell or hell of heaven.'*"

"Man, that's some heavy poetry."

"It's not only heavy, but very profound. The mind is its own place, but it's important that you understand that your thoughts both emanate from your mind and influence future thoughts it generates. Those very thoughts and the emotional force they generate are the determining factors that make a heaven of hell or a hell of heaven in your life. People who are successful tend to predominantly have thoughts of optimism for health, wealth and abundance. That doesn't mean they don't have negative thoughts. Everyone does."

"They do? Positive people have negative thoughts? We just talked about how they build positive thoughts into powerful beliefs."

"Sure, they do. They just don't let them take control of their lives, and they don't allow emotional havoc to set in." Bob reaches over and picks up Bernie's water glass. "They always see the glass as half full. Positive people are also the ultimate *shift-heads*. They create ways to shift their perspective that enable them to use their energy to find solutions rather than wallowing in the problem. They realize when negative thoughts are creeping in and immediately employ tactics to get themselves back on track. They really have their shift together."

"So, what you're really saying is, *when shift happens, your life changes*?"

Bob laughs, swirling the glass of water. "Yes, I guess you could say that. Shifting the way you think leads to beliefs that can bring you more success and happiness."

"Well…I say, 'I think, therefore I have a headache.'"

"It's the way in which you think that causes you problems. All you need to do is to shift your way of thinking. You have the potential to not only know me, but to express yourself through me. In other words, Bernie, the mind is a gateway between people and infinite possibilities. The most important elements in realizing this are in the way they think, what they believe, how they feel and the attitude they have."

"I really have to be careful how I use my thoughts, er…my wand, I guess."

"Absolutely, you do. But especially when you talk with me."

"Are you going to bring me back here often?" asks Bernie with a small lump in this throat.

"I sure hope not!" Bob laughs.

B⛰B's

High Points to Remember

You are not **only human.** *You are my most precious creation. You have no idea of the potential that lies dormant within you. You can create great things. Remember that you are a part of me, and that I am a part of you. You have magical qualities within you."*

B*y allowing yourself to affirm out loud 'I am broke' or 'I don't have enough money,' you are not only choosing to compound the condition in the present, but also into future. If that's what you choose to think, then the universe will respond, 'Well, if that is what you think, then that is what you will get.'"*

P*ositive people are also the ultimate* **shift-heads.** *They create ways to shift their perspective that enable them to use their energy to find solutions rather than wallowing in the problem."*

12

Believe

"Whatever the mind of
man can conceive and
believe, it can achieve."

– NAPOLEON HILL

*B*ernie takes a moment to consider his typical mindset when he prays. *Quiet, humble,* he thinks to himself. *I've always made sure to try to calm down, be respectful. I think I'm doing it right.* After a moment, he says, "As a man thinketh in prayer."

Bob raises an eyebrow. "Ah, so you see where I'm going with this."

Bernie's focus snaps back to Bob. "Uh, yeah, sure," he says. "But I was really just reading from the needlepoint that's hanging behind you."

Bob spins around in his chair and laughs. "Ha! That thing! Betsy Ross made that for me her first week here." He leans forward and says in a low voice, "Honestly, I forgot it was hanging there. You have no idea how profound that statement is. The biggest challenge that people have when they pray is not knowing the crucial role their thoughts, beliefs, feelings and attitudes play. The problem is not that prayers aren't being answered. The problem is that people don't know how important their mindset and emotions are when they pray, or deep inside they don't believe that the prayer will be answered in the first place."

"Hmmm," says Bernie. "So, what you're saying is that many people don't really know or truly understand the basic fundamentals of prayer."

"Exactly! The thing is…when you pray, you are inviting the very essence of who I am to enter the very essence of who you are. It is absolutely a waste of your time to say, *'Hey, Bob, I'm asking for a prayer to be answered, but you know what, I really don't want to take the appropriate action or change my attitude and belief about anything.'* Remember, Universal Law is always working. It doesn't show favorites. It simply works in accordance with what you are thinking, how you are feeling and what you honestly believe."

Bernie closes his mouth and nods.

Bob snaps his fingers and begins to sing. *"And your thought bone is connected to your…belief bone. And your belief bone is connected to your… action bone…"*

Bernie starts bobbing his head in time. "Got it."

"And I will never intervene in how you think and the effects your thoughts have on you. Never! That will always be your choice. Do you understand?"

"I do. That song sure is catchy. What do I need to do to connect all the bones?"

"Okay, first of all, *prayer* is not something that you do for me, but in unity with me so I can do for you."

"So, it's kind of a partnership?"

"Yes. It's not just asking, wanting or hoping. It's certainly not begging or pleading. Instead, it's knowing with an unshakable faith that the prayer has already been answered. In other words, Bernie, I am spirit – pure energy. Therefore, you must always pray to me in spirit. When you pray to me with human qualities of lack or uncertainty, your connection to me is weak, to say the least."

> **"When you pray for a desire to be fulfilled, know that Doubt is the Great Nullifier."**
>
> *– Bob*

"I've got to give up my humanity to reach you?" Bernie asks.

"Not entirely. Yes, it's true that you're more than just human. To aspire to be your best self, as a human, is part of the great plan. It's a part of me. But your spirit is what matters. That's why you must always go into prayer in spirit from the higher part of yourself. It's not what I must do for you. It is what you must do for yourself to enable me to do for you." Bob looks over at Bernie. "Are you getting this?"

"I think so. Let me see if I got this right. When it comes to a prayer being answered, it's really not what you can do for me, but what you can do *through* me. And that is always my responsibility. It's up to me to make the connection."

"Yes, yes! That's it! Answered prayers or miracles are your right, Bernie, no matter what you want to call them. But you have to cleanse yourself. You have to work at throwing out the garbage in your mind in order to make the connection. A prayer has to go through you – *your consciousness* – in accordance with how you think, believe and feel and the overall attitude you have. When you pray, you have to leave doubt out of the equation."

"Once again, it's all about faith," says Bernie.

"Bernie, I can't express to you enough how important that word is! Faith is key! Faith is the great miracle-working power. Faith is the intangible force that comes to the rescue when your beliefs begin to falter."

"My mom used to say that faith is knowing there is light even when you are surrounded by nothing but darkness."

"Your mother was truly a wise person, Bernie."

Bernie smiles. "Yes…yes, she was. Unlike my father, my mother always saw the light at the end of the tunnel. She always saw the glass as half full."

"Yes, she did," says Bob.

Bernie pauses to reflect. "Wow, Bob, I just had a flashback to when I was in high school. I was very confused as to what I wanted to do with my life. I mean, I was really upset…my mom looked straight into my eyes and told me I had the whole world at my command…that I could create miracles if I wanted to…if I allowed them to happen."

Bob looks Bernie straight in the eyes and says, "That's why you always have to keep the faith."

"Yeah," says Bernie. "At the time, I thought it was just a pep talk. I didn't grasp the meaning of what she was trying to convey to me. After all these years, I now understand."

Bob gives Bernie a tissue and a moment to harness his emotions. "Are you okay, Bernie?"

Bernie wipes a tear from his eye and takes a deep breath. "Yeah, Bob, I'm okay."

Bob leans back in his chair, puts his feet on top of the desk and his hands behind his head and says, "Sometimes learning life's lessons can be a hard pill to swallow. Especially when they take a long time to learn."

Bernie shakes his head. "You got that right, Bob."

"Of course, I got that right! I'm Bob Almighty! I always get it right! *ALL-WAYS!*"

Bernie laughs. "Oh brother! Talk about having an inflated ego!"

"Ha!" says Bob. "Me having an ego! Now that's funny! Humor…I absolutely love what I created! Shall we continue our conversation?"

"Go for it, Bob."

"It's crucial that you speak to me not so much in words, but in the language that my energy field, the universe, the Divine Matrix or whatever you choose to call it recognizes and understands."

"Okay," Bernie says. "What language is that? And how do I do that?"

Just then, the chalkboard rolls from the far end of the room and stops short on the side of Bob's desk, followed by a piece of chalk. The chalk is floating in midair, waiting for Bob to speak.

Bob responds to Bernie's question in a slow, methodical manner as his words are written simultaneously on the board. "By evoking thoughts and ideas of elation…and marrying those thoughts and ideas with the emotions they elicit." Bob waits as Bernie contemplates.

Bernie mumbles to himself. "By evoking thoughts of elation and…marry my emotions…? I'm sorry, Bob, can you elaborate a little bit more?"

"Okay," says Bob. "Listen…It cannot be stressed enough that my energy field does not recognize your inner voice nearly as much as it recognizes the energy of your heart's desire. Words, thoughts or ideas without exhilarating feeling and emotion to support them are bland and simply do not have enough bandwidth to connect to my frequency. They dramatically slow down – stifle – the transmission process to my energy field."

Bob pauses and looks directly at Bernie. He continues speaking in the same methodical manner as the chalk follows along.

"When you allow high-powered-thoughts…ideas and words of elation…to merge with the emotions they elicit…they become one potent-euphoric-force within your heart. When this happens…you create a surge of high-powered-euphoric feelings throughout your entire body. Those high-powered-euphoric feelings of confidence and certainty are the language my energy field recognizes and responds to."

Bernie ponders for a moment. "So…I need to communicate with thoughts and ideas that create feelings of positivity?"

"Well…yes…but it's more than that," says Bob. "When you ask for something in prayer, you must not only *see it in your mind's eye*, but you must *feel it from your heart* with utter certainty that the prayer is answered. This is crucial, Bernie! *Feeling is the prayer!*"

"Ask and you shall receive kind of thing," says Bernie.

"Yes!" Says Bob. "But in order to receive, you have to become enveloped by your idea…your desire…as if it already happened, without judgment…without ego. You must believe and feel that the thing you are asking for is already a fact…that it's there in existence, even though you can't see it or touch it in your physical world. Remember what we said about faith."

> *"Ask and you shall receive…Visualize and it will Materialize…Believe and you will Achieve. It's the LAW!"*
>
> – *Bob*

"I remember," says Bernie. "But there within lies the rub. I mean, it's very difficult for people to grasp the concept or the reality of *believe it and you'll see it*. To be honest, I have a difficult time with it."

Bob feels the conflict within Bernie's humanity. "Bernie, my dear friend. *Believe it and you'll see it* is not just a phrase or a concept! And it certainly is not an escape from reality! In fact, it is tuning into the *ultimate reality!* I am far more *Real* than the world you can see, hear and touch."

Bernie feels the intensity and compassion radiating from Bob.

Suddenly, Bob snaps his fingers and the chalk whizzes by Bernie's nose. As Bob speaks, the chalk writes. *"Believe it and you'll see it is a hard-core confirmation of things you do not yet see in your physical world and the conviction of their reality."*

Just then, Bob snaps his fingers. "I have an idea!"

Bernie smiles. "Uh-oh. You gonna create another planet or universe or something?"

"Nope," says Bob. "Been there, done that."

"Should I duck under the desk?" Bernie says jokingly.

"Very funny," says Bob. "I'm going to show you step by step the formula for prayer…on how to create and speak the true language that my energy field will recognize and understand. After which, you will have no problem understanding what I mean when I say, *'Believe it and you'll see it.'*"

"Really?" says Bernie.

"Really," says Bob.

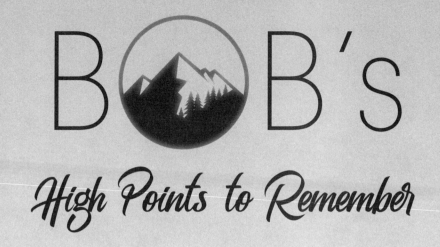

BOB's

High Points to Remember

*P*rayer is not just asking, wanting or hoping. It's certainly not begging or pleading. Instead, it's knowing with an unshakable faith that the prayer has already been answered."

*Y*ou must always go into prayer in spirit from the higher part of yourself. It's not what I must do for you. It is what you must do for yourself to enable me to do for you."

A prayer has to go through you – your consciousness – in accordance with how you think, believe and feel and the overall attitude you have. When you pray, you have to leave human qualities of doubt and lack out of the equation."

*F*aith is key! Faith is the great miracle-working power. Faith is the intangible force that comes to the rescue when your beliefs begin to falter."

Part 4

"This, my friend, is your place of refuge.
Know that in this place resides a World
of Infinite Possibilities, where you can
choose – and together we can fulfill –
the life you desire."

– Bob

In this transformative finale, Bernie learns how to...

▶ Implement the *Formula for Prayer* into his daily life.

▶ Manage the *Dominant Toxic Beliefs* that are etched in stoned deep within the caverns of his mind.

▶ Stop the destructive *"Big Mouth"* voice track inside his head from creating havoc in his life.

▶ Embrace the most Powerful Force in the Universe.

13

The Formula

> "No matter what, never underestimate the power of prayer, love and faith."
>
> — ANURAG PRAKASH RAY

*S*uddenly, the entire room turns pitch black. "Wow!" says Bernie. "Did you forget to pay the electric bill? Bernie gets no response. "Bob…Hey, Bob. Are you still there?"

There is a moment of silence before Bob speaks. His voice has taken on a soothing, hypnotic quality that captivates Bernie's attention immediately.

"I'm still here, Bernie. I want you to do exactly as I instruct. Got it?"

"Got it, Bob," Bernie says softly.

"Close your eyes," Bob's voice says. "Sit up straight in your chair, spread your legs slightly apart with your feet flat on the floor and place your hands on your lap."

Bernie complies.

Bob continues. "Now, take deep breaths in through your nose and exhale through your mouth. *In….out…in…out…*"

Bernie continues breathing for a few moments.

Bob's voice continues in a slow, methodical tone. "Bernie…I am going to give you one of many ways to get into the right frame of mind for prayer. Whatever way you choose, it's essential that you give yourself significant time somewhere alone, where you will not be disturbed."

Bob senses that Bernie is getting in the right frame of mind.

Bob continues. "Since you are a lover of nature and I am most revealed in nature, I want you to envision yourself sitting on a front porch of a house, on the beach of your own private habitat called Bernie Island. Allow yourself to take in the glorious view of the sun slowly settling over the ocean. Feel the stillness…see the…beauty… the colors. Hear the quite harmonic sounds of nature…the song of the birds…the waves rolling on the shore. Embrace the magnificence of what I have created and what you are experiencing."

Bob waits to allow Bernie's vision to take root.

"This, my friend, is your sacred place of refuge. Know that here in this sacred place resides a World of Infinite Possibilities, where you can choose and together we can fulfill the life you desire." Bob senses that Bernie is totally immersed in his sacred place of refuge. "Bernie, right now I want you to shift your attention to what we were discussing before about the things you claim aren't working in your life. It is important that you simply acknowledge what is, without Ego, without judgment. Do not view it as good or bad, right or wrong, fair or unfair. Simply view it as one of the many possibilities that exist in the World of Infinite Possibilities."

Bob pauses to make sure that Bernie is just acknowledging and not judging.

"Good…Very good," says Bob. "Now, I want you to gradually shift your focus away from the possibility of lack and decide that you're simply going to choose another possibility."

Bob pauses until Bernie does as he suggests.

Bob continues. "Now…envision yourself reaching into this wonderful World of Infinite Possibilities with your mind." Bob pauses. "Now…identify and then choose the possibility that fulfills your heart's desire and lock onto it."

Bob smiles as he sees the possibility that Bernie has chosen.

"Bernie, right now, I want you to kick your thought process…this possibility that you have chosen…into high gear. It's time to have some fun and elaborate on the life that you truly desire. I want you to focus and get into this. Do not hold back. Know that I am with you as you go through this process. Know that we are always, always creating together the things you desire."

> *"Pray is not flattery, but a sense of oneness with Me. It's not asking, but knowing. It's not words, but feeling...I'm just saying."*
>
> *– Bob*

Bob gives Bernie time to relax to conjure up his vision and focus on the life he desires. Then, he slowly and methodically continues. "Allow yourself to see every detail of what your new ideal life looks and feels like. View it as if someone is showing you a video highlight of what you have created. I mean, see and feel every detail. See yourself smiling as you go through your day. See yourself doing the things you love to do...purchasing things you desire."

Bob pauses to allow Bernie's vision to flourish. "Feel your new-found confidence...the shift in your attitude throughout the day in your business and in life. Know that there will be challenges along the way, but also know that there is a part of you that can meet any challenge head on...that there is a solution to every problem. Feel the power of that. Feel the certainty of living the dream fulfilled. Feel the respect you have for yourself and get from others...see yourself helping those who are in need."

Bob pauses again for a few moments to allow Bernie to experience the life he has chosen and truly desires. "Bernie, are you witnessing the life desired? Can you feel the wish fulfilled?"

"Yes, Bob," Bernie says emotionally. "I can...this is really a trip. I feel as if I'm in some kind of time warp...I can see and feel every detail! Holy crap, Bob. I can even see in colors! I feel like I'm going to burst with emotion!"

Bob smiles and senses that Bernie is nearing the high point of his manifestation process. "Now…allow your vision and those thoughts of elation to merge with the emotions they elicit…and feel that potent force permeate your heart with every fiber of your being! Really…really…feel this, Bernie. Feel the sensation of that potent force fill your heart!"

"Oh my…Bob!" Bernie blurts out softly.

Bob feels the euphoric, emotional energy radiating from Bernie. "Now…release the force, the feeling from within your heart, and allow it to permeate your entire body. Feel it with your very soul! Embrace the harmony! Feel the Joy! See yourself entering the home of your dreams. See yourself walking into every room of your beautiful house. Notice the colors of the walls, the furniture and the wonderful neighborhood you live in. Envision yourself relaxing…sitting in your favorite chair watching television and barbecuing in your beautiful backyard entertaining friends. Feel the Love from the result of the things we created! Give thanks to it! Own it!"

At this point, Bernie is a total mass of emotions. Bob gives him more time for the creation process to evolve, then continues. "See yourself pulling out of your driveway in your new car. Give thanks for it! Know that it is so! See and feel the magnificence you have created, that we have created together. Say to yourself, 'I chose this! I took action and met every challenge head on! This is real! It is done… Thank you! It is done!'"

Bernie repeats in an emotional whisper, "I chose this! I took action and met every challenge head on! This is real! It is done…Thank you! It is done!"

"Trust the process, Bernie! Acknowledge and feel the power of Love within you! Give thanks again and again! Own it with your heart and soul! For you truly are the creator of your success and happiness!"

Just then, the lights come back on. Bernie is sitting speechless and overwhelmed with emotions in front of Bob's desk.

"Tada!" says Bob enthusiastically. "And that, my friend, is the language my energy field recognizes."

Bernie is sitting motionless, transfixed in a wave of emotions. "I...will never...ever...be able to explain what just happened to me!" says Bernie.

"Don't even try. It's like I said: sometimes words get in the way. The important thing is the elation you felt through the entire experience."

"Yes," Bernie replies, in awe. "I actually feel invincible! I now understand the process of how my thoughts and my ideas of elation merge with my emotions and become one potent force with my heart." Bernie contemplates. "And as soon as I allowed that to happen, Bob, I felt an explosion...a power surge of potent energy flowing from my heart, through my entire body. I've never felt anything like that before! The more I visualized it, the more intense and real it became!"

"Exactly!" says Bob. "Use that process every time you want a desire fulfilled, regardless of what it is. Remember, Bernie, the endless wealth and abundance of the universe will be yours to the degree that you can *See* it in your mind's eye, *Feel* it in your heart and *Believe* that it is so and take action accordingly."

Bernie contemplates what Bob just said. "So...if I have a presentation to give at work or an idea to propose, I should envision myself communicating with confidence, passion and enthusiasm... envision the process...see the end result of that desire...of people enthusiastically shaking my hand and patting me on the back and telling me I did a great job and envision the fruits of my labor."

"Absolutely!" says Bob. "Whether your goal is to write a book or create a loving relationship, a healthy body or a prosperous business. See your creation happening in your mind's eye…feel the momentum building and allow those thoughts and ideas of elation to merge with your emotions, which in turn will become one potent force within your heart and, as you stated, feel the explosion of that force flowing through your entire body!"

"Amazing!" says Bernie. "Simply amazing and miraculous!"

"Miraculous indeed. But…" Bob pauses and points a finger at Bernie. "You have to live those feelings throughout the day…Every day. This is not something you do for a few moments in prayer and then get up and walk away. It's about clarity. It's about taking action and living the dream fulfilled every day regardless of what's transpiring around you."

"I hear you, Bob," says Bernie. "Keep the momentum going throughout the day. Every day. As I'm creating the life I desire, it's my responsibility not to focus on my current situation of lack…the things that aren't working…to keep thoughts of doubt and failure out of the equation."

"That's very wise of you," says Bob. "Any limitation must be a limitation in the thoughts you have, the words you speak and in the faith that shapes the substance."

"Got it." Says Bernie.

Bob continues. "It's also important that you eliminate any words in your vocabulary that demonstrate hesitancy regarding the things you desire. Be careful how you entertain thoughts and use words like *maybe, hopefully,* and *possibly*."

"Why?" asks Bernie.

"Because these words indicate uncertainty," says Bob.

Bernie thinks for a moment. "Oh…I get it. So, if I were to say, '*I hope I give a great presentation today,*' that leaves room for doubt to seep through and suggests that it might not ever happen."

"Exactly. It would be best if you were to say, '*I always attract what I desire. I'm so excited that I'm going to give a great presentation today. I got this!*'"

"And, of course, visualize accordingly," says Bernie.

"Absolutely!" says Bob. "And remember, my friend, always replace doubt with an attitude of gratitude. When you feel your desires might not make their way to you, or whenever you're feeling insecure about your manifestation process, simply make a conscious effort to nip the doubtful thoughts in the bud and replace them with thoughts of gratitude. This will retrain your mind, your subconscious, away from uncertainty and help you focus on the fact that you have already manifested many wonderful things for yourself."

Bernie contemplates and says, "So…my thought process… positive or negative…is the key factor to the image I choose from the World of Infinite Possibilities?"

"Bingo!" says Bob. "You see, in the World of Infinite Possibilities, everything already exists. Your life of financial lack and your life of financial abundance. Your perfect relationship and the worst one you will ever have. Your greatest healing and your greatest suffering. And so on."

Bernie places his hands on top of his head and speaks. "Wow, Bob, I truly am the creator of my success and happiness."

Bob smiles. "Yes, Bernie, you truly are. That's why it's crucial that you never allow your current circumstances to interfere with your heart's desire. If your heart is consumed with feelings of doubt, uncertainty, fear and other Destroyers of the Spirit, you will stop or drastically slow down the manifestation process of your desire. This is why most people get frustrated and stop believing, and eventually quit and give up on their dreams. You have to monitor your thoughts and emotions every day, throughout the day."

Bernie shakes his head in approval. "Because negative thoughts will merge with the emotions *they* elicit and create a dysphoric force of energy within my heart, which in turn will elicit more feelings of lack, doubt, victimization and a host of other Destroyers of the Spirit."

"Right you are!" says Bob. "My energy field, aka. *The Law of Attraction*, will respond accordingly because it always gives you what you ask for – whether you want it or not."

"Got it," says Bernie. "The more I focus on my lack, the more of that I will get back."

The Universal Scheme of Things

"And…last, but not least." Bob raises his eyebrow as he stares at Bernie. "You have to trust that it will happen in the universal scheme of things. Not when *you* think it *should* happen."

"Why are you giving me that look?"

"Oh," says Bob. "Sorry. Was I looking at you like you're a toddler again? It's because you are very impatient. You have a tendency to wait a few days, or maybe even weeks, before asking, *'When is it going to happen?'* When you respond like this, you're sending a message to the universe that you haven't arrived at the place of trust and that your desires are already an eventuality waiting to happen. In other words, you're questioning the status of your desires. You are actually slowing down the transmission, the process of their fulfillment, because you've allowed your ego to dictate a time of arrival. Not to mention the doubt and other negative stuff that evolves as you're waiting. This is counterproductive. You're setting up resistance instead of just allowing the universal mind that uses my energy field to bring you what you desire at the appropriate time."

"It seems to me that, in principle, prayer is quite simple," Bernie says. "but, more often than not, the human side of us interferes with the mechanics of how prayer works."

"Remember, dear reader, the Formula for prayer is universally applicable in all places, at all times, and for all persons, including you."

– Bob

"Yeah," says Bob. "The universe is strangely bureaucratic that way. When you start having doubt and complaining, you move to the back of the line again. It's true your humanity poses an obstacle, but remember who you are…"

Now Bernie nods and interrupts. "I know, Bob. *I am more than just human.*"

"Yep. Speaking of which, another common human reaction you have that slows down the manifestation process is when you predetermine *how* your desires will come to pass. Not only does it wreck your ability to live in the moment, it screws up your chances to recognize when great future, unknown opportunities and moments are presenting themselves."

"Whoa," Bernie says. *"Double whammy."*

"Double whammy, indeed. It's generated by the ego's yearning to control the outcome. The problem with this is that the ego is incredibly limited. It only knows the range of what you know and experience, which doesn't even begin to compare to the vast possibilities that are way beyond your imagination. Sorry for the toddler crack earlier, but it's an easy analogy to make. What kinds of dreams for your future did you have when you were five years old?"

"Honestly," says Bernie, "I wanted to live in my treehouse. I think I had vague ideas of becoming a lumberjack. Or a pirate."

"That's because the information you had at the time pales in comparison to the information you have now. Take the information you have currently as a grown adult, multiply that by an unimaginable figure, and you'll see how little you know right now about the possibilities of the universe and what would work for you."

"I see. I had no clue about the world then. And I guess I still don't."

"The result of fixating on the exact path is that you become attached to the one outcome you believe or want to transpire. You overlook the amazing opportunities that the universe is offering you."

Bernie gets it. "Like the way I ignored the guy on the plane?"

"Yes! He very well could have been an opportunity that the universe was offering you. But you should also know that a seed possibility could very well be just the beginning of a long, challenging and tedious process. A great many steps may need to be taken before the desire is fully manifested."

"What do you mean?" asks Bernie.

"The guy on the plane might have been the cosmic piece that set things moving. He, in turn, could have introduced you to someone else who had more knowledge and clout. This person could have set up a meeting with a group of experts for you to demonstrate your idea. They may have loved your idea but found some glitches or flaws that needed to be improved, which would mean that you would have to go back to the drawing board again."

Bernie's face starts to fall with every step that Bob lists.

"Then you would have to set up another meeting to prove all of the glitches were fixed. And just when you think everything is ready to go, there could be a disagreement as to the percentage you were going to get or a hassle with the patent laws. I don't have to tell you what happens when attorneys get involved. Lawyers! I said the universe is bureaucratic! This entire process could take weeks, months or years before everything comes together."

Bernie takes a deep breath. "Gee, Bob, there could be a number of time-consuming scenarios that take place. Isn't it understandable that someone could get lost or distracted along the way?"

"Life is a process, Bernie. Remember?"

Bernie nods. "Yes, *and the process is my life.*"

"But you see, it doesn't necessarily mean your prayers aren't being answered. It simply means they haven't manifested yet. What's important for you to understand is to keep the faith during the entire process. I mean *every* step along the way. That's your choice and responsibility. You have to keep your connection to me strong."

"Sounds like a pretty constant deal."

Bob smiles. "Keep the faith and positivity going, my friend! Every day, be enveloped by what you desire. See it in your mind's eye and feel it in your heart as if it already happened! I can't tell you how many people have quit pursuing their dreams just when they were so close to making them happen. And…," Bob says, leaning in to Bernie, "be very aware that miracles, as you call them, will often come to you first as an idea…a creative impulse."

"Just like our three inventors," Bernie says.

"Yes," says Bob. "Always be on the lookout for the serendipitous events that will no doubt occur when you are on track and tuned into my frequency. These events often take place in subtle ways. They quite often take place when you casually ask yourself questions that begin with *How come...?* or *How can I...?* or *What if...?* Be aware because the answer can come at any time and from anywhere. There are countless ways that serendipity can take place. No matter what form it comes in, it's all part of the miraculous process."

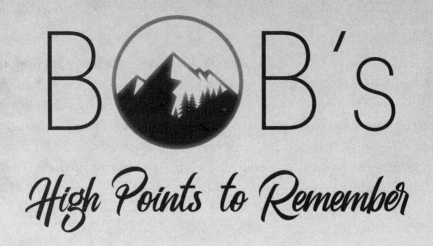

B O B's

High Points to Remember

*B*elieve it and you'll see **it is not just a phrase or a concept! It** *is a hard-core confirmation of things you do not yet see in your physical world and the conviction of their reality."*

*S*ee your creation happening in your mind's eye...feel the *momentum building and allow those thoughts and ideas of elation to merge with your emotions, which in turn will become one potent force within your heart and, feel the explosion of that force flowing through your entire body!"*

*I*n the World of Infinite Possibilities, *everything already exists. Your life of financial lack and your life of financial abundance. Your perfect relationship and the worst one you will ever have. Your greatest healing and your greatest suffering. And so on."*

14

Dominant Toxic Beliefs

"Our beliefs are like unquestioned commands, telling us how things are, what's possible and impossible and what we can and cannot do. They shape every action, every thought and every feeling that we experience."

– TONY ROBBINS

"Thanks, Bob. I get it." Bernie resists the urge to look at his watch. He senses he might get a second chance to put his new understanding into practice, and he's *excited*. "Okay, is there anything else I need to know?"

"Yes, in fact, there is. But we're going to be getting into some challenging and complicated stuff here. Are you ready to listen to what I have to say, no matter what?"

Bernie breathes deeply. He tamps down his eagerness to focus on the future. It would make sense to learn every last bit he could while he is here. "I think so."

"Even if you muster up all of the positive thinking and confidence you can in a moment of prayer, or when you're setting out to achieve a goal, it will still be very difficult to override the dominant negative thoughts and toxic beliefs that have been built up for a lifetime. Do you know what I'm getting at?"

Bernie grimaces. "Maybe? Tell me more."

Bob leans back and laces his hands behind his head. "Okay, I'm going to give you a crude but effective metaphor to illustrate once again how a constant trend in your thoughts can grow into beliefs. Several years ago, you went with a few friends to climb Mt. Rainier in Washington."

"Yes! How did you…Oh, well, yeah. Of course. It was an amazing experience!"

Bob laughs. "I know, I know. The place where that mountain lies has been a pool of magma, a deep sea, a lush rainforest. All these manifestations have taken eons to shape."

"Is this about how each took time and billions of tiny subtle movements of Earth to form? I saw a pretty great documentary about that the other day…"

"Nope," Bob says, cutting Bernie short. "It's about your diet and mindset…how you're feeding your soul and mind. Tell me about how you prepared for that trip."

Bernie seems thrown off. "Uh, well, um. I can't really remember. You saw it all, apparently. Will you refresh my memory?"

"Of course. Almost seven months before your adventure, you stopped eating junk food. You were worried that David and James, with all of their CrossFit bragging, would think you were growing soft, which you were. However, instead of ordering cheeseburgers or pizza, you ordered salads, grilled chicken and vegetables and drank protein shakes. You hired a trainer and exercised daily. You were actually getting back in shape. Not just physically, but mentally, emotionally and, might I say, *spiritually*."

"Well, the preparation materials they sent laid out a pretty good roadmap for getting ready. Physically, mentally, emotionally…and, to be honest, Bob, I didn't realize I was getting in shape spiritually."

"Yet that's what you did. And you followed it all pretty well. Do you remember what you thought when you reached the summit of that mountain?"

Bernie swallows. His mouth is dry. "I thought, '*I can do anything*,'" he croaks. "And I thought, '*I want to do even more*,' and I believed that I could."

Bob takes his hands from behind his head and puts them down on the desk in front of him. To Bernie, this action seems to take as long as it took for a mountain to form and eventually crumble.

"What happened after your adventure?" asks Bob.

"Oh…life, I guess," says Bernie. "You get back to the same old routine. You get back to comfort…the hustle and bustle, the worries, you know? It's hard to live extraordinarily all the time."

Bob nods and shakes his head at the same time, so his face looks briefly like he is watching a fly buzz around the room. "No. Yes. It is hard to live extraordinarily, but it is also not. It seems funny to me that one of the quintessential human endeavors – climbing a mountain – elicits such emotional and physical commitments. Poets have often invoked the spirit of the mountain as something that is man's unique endeavor or, heck, responsibility. After all, it is the most tangible way, they think, of becoming close to the heavens. Closer to me. Amazing."

"It was pretty great, Bob," says Bernie.

"The point I'm trying to make," says Bob, "is that the commitment you made to a brief goal was incredible. That commitment…your determination…on a consistent daily basis was exactly what was needed to become closer to me – to connect to my energy field. Your positivity was pretty high. It flew against all the usual negative tendencies and toxic habits you've built up over the years. Like worrying and doubting yourself…to avoid getting back in shape, to eat poorly or raid the mini-bar. You'll always like pizza, right?"

Bernie nods emphatically.

"And right now, even after all that you've learned throughout this conversation, you still have a trace of doubt. There's still a touch of worry as to whether you will be able to apply the strategies I offered you. Am I right?"

"Remember…just one Negative Thought can snowball into an Avalanche of negative emotions."

– Bob

Bernie nods again, a little more slowly.

"That's because those toxic mindsets and beliefs are set in stone, lingering in the back of your mind with all of the other negative beliefs and habits you've created throughout your life. Why do you think you chose to change your behavior for that period of time when climbing the mountain?"

"Well, clearly, I didn't want to embarrass myself in front of my friends. Plus, the mountain was a tangible goal. I mean, I knew what needed to be done. There was a clear timetable. Positive steps needed to be taken, and I had to get moving, and that's exactly what I did. Come to think of it, it was like I was on automatic pilot. I was determined. I was free from distractions or doubt. I really didn't even think about failing. To top it all off, I had a blast! There were times when we laughed our asses off! I managed to forge ahead and actually enjoyed the entire process in spite of the difficulties."

"The point is you took the necessary positive steps to achieve that one goal. You were focused and, as you just said, you didn't allow any distractions or doubt to interfere with what you set out to do. You were in the moment. You were enjoying the entire process. For the first time in a long time, you had a profound appreciation for being alive. Do you see what I'm getting at?"

Bernie, once again, feels his widening midsection.

"Bernie…it is your cumulative positive thoughts and beliefs throughout your life that will bring you continued opportunities for triumphs like the one you experienced when you tapped into the spirit of the mountain."

"So…if I had continued in the same mindset of achieving the one goal of climbing the mountain, I might be in contention for achieving others I have no idea are on the horizon?"

"Yes," Bob says. "It is your continuing mindset that matters. Whether positive or negative, it is the majority of hardcore dominating beliefs that are engraved deep within the caverns in your mind that are writing the story of your life. You've spent a lifetime thinking, believing and feeling in one way, which wasn't productive, to say the least. Do you think just a few months of behaving differently, of thinking positively, will make much of a difference in your life in the long run?"

Bernie takes a deep breath in and out. "I guess not."

> "Stop and ask yourself: 'Are my beliefs writing a story of abundance and joy? Or are they writing a story of scarcity and despair?'"
>
> – Bob

"Remember, your beliefs are shaped by a regular, consistent way of thinking. Positive, productive thoughts will create positive beliefs that will allow you to overcome obstacles, to learn from mistakes and to move forward to achieve success. Let's call those beliefs health food for the soul or grilled chicken. On the other hand, if your beliefs are shaped by a bombardment of negative streams of thoughts, a toxic, self-limiting belief system will be created. Unfortunately, in your case, those beliefs are the majority, and they're crippling you mentally, emotionally, physically and spiritually. Let's call those cheeseburgers or junk food for the soul."

"I guess this really isn't about my diet?"

"This is about how you feed your mind and soul in order to achieve what you want, Bernie."

Bernie thinks for a moment. "So...my training to climb the mountain was successful because it was tangible. I was totally focused.

I didn't leave room for fear or doubt or any other negative thoughts to seep through and take control. I was aimed at achieving success and, as a result, that's what I did. Even though it was challenging, I still managed to forge ahead and enjoy the entire process."

"Yes, but unfortunately, that represents the small moments in life where you concentrated on consistent positive thinking. The rest of the time is your distraction. In other words, your positive thoughts in the moment of your prayer time, or when you're setting out to achieve a goal, are more often than not overridden by your dominant toxic beliefs that have been solidified over a lifetime of junk food for the soul and mind."

"And those fleeting positive thoughts really don't stand much of a chance against a lifetime of dominant toxic beliefs that I have created," Bernie says.

"And a pizza sounds great right about now," Bob says. "Mind if I order one?"

"Holy Shit! I mean 'Shift!' *Holy Shift!*" Bernie slaps a hand over his mouth. "Sorry, I didn't mean to curse. I got carried away. Please continue."

"No need to apologize. I'm not offended."

"You don't get offended when people swear? You're as cool as I'd hoped."

"Contrary to what many people think, no, I don't get offended. Words themselves have no intention, no danger. They're sounds, that's all."

"Aw hell, that's great! So, it's okay to swear?"

"Swearing can't offend me, but it can cause great damage when you use it against each other. When standing alone, what you call a 'swear' or 'curse' word is just that, it's merely a word and nothing more. It's the way in which people use or manipulate words towards each other that makes them vulgar and destructive. It's when a word is spewed out towards someone in conjunction with venom, anger or even hatred that it can cause great damage. Not only to the person being cursed, but also to the person who is doing the cursing. Words and the emotions that fuel them have the power to create or destroy."

"So, I guess I should be careful about what I say and how I say it?"

"You got that right. But let's get back to what we were discussing before you get sidetracked to hell and back."

"So, all I have to do is get rid of the unproductive dominant beliefs?"

"Well...yes...and no. What I mean is...you can't really get rid of your dominant negative beliefs. As I stated earlier, they're set in stone. They will always be with you, lingering in the background of your mind, ready to strike and do damage."

"Well, that doesn't sound very promising."

"Actually, it is very promising. In fact, it's very empowering. Here's an opportunity for you to grow and to use the *Power of Choice* to your advantage. Bernie, you can choose to be vigilant and become aware when those toxic beliefs are about to strike. You can also choose to ignore them and not to feed them more negative thoughts. If you do this, your dominant negative beliefs will remain stagnant and harmless. But always be aware and vigilant, Bernie, because they are always ready to strike. Remember that is your choice and responsibility to keep them at bay. Just one negative thought in the moment can create a rampage of like thoughts and ill feelings that will attack with a vengeance. Thoughts are the most powerful triggers."

"Let me make sure I've got this right. Before, during and after I pray, or whenever I make a decision or set out to achieve anything throughout the day, I have to be aware and make certain that I don't feed those dominant negative beliefs that are lingering in that particular cavern in my mind."

"Yes, and what I'm asking you to do now, Bernie, is to create healthier, optimistic and productive dominant thoughts and beliefs to counteract the toxic, fear-based ones that have been dominating your life so far. Once you've accomplished this, you can pretty much have more control over your life because positive beliefs will allow your light to shine. Your light is your connection to me. When you are connected to me…well…let's just say that fear, no matter what form it comes in, cannot stand against me."

Bernie gets an incredulous look on his face as a faint glow of light begins to emanate from Bob as he closes his eyes and declares in a voice that seems to echo through the cosmos…

"That's not bragging…*just fact.*"

B O B's

High Points to Remember

Keep the faith going. I mean every step along the way. Everyday be enveloped by what you desire. I can't tell you how many people have quit pursuing their dreams just when they were so close to making them happen."

Whether positive or negative, it is the majority of hardcore dominating beliefs that are engraved deep within the caverns in your mind that are writing the story of your life."

You can choose to be vigilant and become aware when toxic beliefs are about to strike. You can also choose to ignore them and not to feed them more negative thoughts. If you do this, your dominant negative beliefs will remain stagnant and harmless."

15

Self-Curse-Talk

> "If there is anything that keeps people from being productive and happy and partaking in the abundance that life has to offer, it's Self-Curse-Talk."
>
> – BOB (THE ONE AND ONLY!)

s the illumination begins to subside, Bob rises and bustles around his office, selecting items and returning to line them up in a row, including a small globe of Earth, the endless hourglass, an ordinary stapler and a small wooden box.

Bernie is in awe. "Wow! Did you see that serious light show thing? What was that? Incredible! Okay, I'm ready. How do I do this?"

Bob smiles, and as the last remnants of light dissipate from his form, he continues speaking.

"Once again, by creating new habits. You see, Bernie, positive thoughts, beliefs and feelings mean very little unless you make it a habit to focus your attention on them throughout the day. Every day!"

"Just like focusing on the things I'm grateful for so I can create the habit of feeling good and enjoying the process."

"Yes. As you are well aware by now, you have a long history of thoughts and beliefs that have created a field of resistance that kept the flow of abundance from coming into your life."

Bernie takes a deep breath. "Yes, I am well aware of that."

"Well," says Bob, "what you're probably not aware of is that you aided that field of resistance by letting the opinions of others create your worldview of things. You even went so far as to allow some of them to tell you what was right for you, what decisions to make and what they thought would make you happy."

"I did?" says Bernie. "Really?"

"Really," Bob replies. "And through the years, in one way or another, you've conditioned yourself with the need for their approval.

At times, you actually sought out their resistant point of view. For example, you consistently read, and take to heart, all the negative newspaper headlines and TV news shows that financially profit from spewing out the sad state of affairs in the world. However, most damaging of all is when you allowed the opinions of family members, friends, teachers and business associates to literally crush your ideas and dreams before they even had a chance to take root. Not only did you not have trust and faith in yourself to allow abundance to come into your life, but you put your trust and faith in the hands of others. In other words, my friend, you have aligned yourself with the proponents of disallowing the things you desired."

Bernie looks dumbfounded. "Oh, wow, Bob! I had no idea!"

"I know you didn't, Bernie. Very few people are aware of what they're doing to themselves."

"The key is to become aware and learn the lesson." says Bernie.

"Exactly" says Bob. "The toxic beliefs you are harboring now were formulated over a period of time by habitual negative thinking. What I'm asking you to do is to gradually, methodically and continuously shift the way you think to positive and productive habits that will instill faith, confidence and trust in yourself. It's especially important that you understand you are not only the producer of your thoughts, but also the director."

"The only losers in the game of life are those who, for whatever reason, fail to use their challenges as a springboard for growth."

– Bob

Bob picks up the wooden box in front of him and opens it. A light shines up from within.

"In any given circumstance," he says, "you have the power to use your mind to create feel-good thoughts that will propel you to view any situation from a higher part of yourself – from an advantage rather than a disadvantage. The more you do this, the more you solidify a healthier belief system. Think of your mind as a box from which you can summon powerful transforming thoughts at will."

"Boy, that's one hell of a responsibility," says Bernie.

"It sure as hell is, but it's also heavenly to know that you may not be able to change what's happening to you, yet you can always choose how you think about what happens. How you think about what happens eventually leads to the actions you take."

"And, once again, the actions I take will lead me to a particular outcome."

"You are on a roll, my man!" Bob places the box into a briefcase by his desk, then reaches out and turns the hourglass. "Remember, Bernie, taking action without Passion and Enthusiasm is merely going through the motions. You have an unbelievably small amount of time on Earth. You can't even begin to fathom how to fully experience all the things that matter to you and to everyone around you."

Bob gives the small globe a spin. "Climbing mountains is just the beginning."

"I know, Bob. Enjoyment is the spark that ignites Passion and Enthusiasm. And enjoyment is my choice and responsibility."

"Attaboy. When you realize how much control you have over your own life, you'll realize how far-reaching the influence of your presence and attitude truly are." Bob places the globe into the briefcase.

Bernie is practically bouncing in his seat. "So, Bob, let's start the habit-forming process that will override my dominant, fear-based, negative beliefs and replace them with a healthier, more productive belief system."

"First of all, you have to stop the *Self-Curse-Talk* in your everyday life – because you are taking that mindset with you everywhere you go."

"*Self-Curse-Talk?*"

"Some call it *Negative-Self-Talk* or something along those lines. I call it *Self-Curse-Talk* because this type of internal dialogue literally curses you with its power to cast a spell on your life." Bob slumps in his seat and affects a pitch-perfect impression of Bernie: "*'This isn't going to work. I can't believe how stupid I am. This happens every time I try to think outside the box.'* Sound familiar?"

Bernie cringes. "Do I really sound like that?"

"No, not at all. You sound worse than that. If there is anything that keeps people from being productive and happy and partaking in the abundance that life has to offer, it's *Self-Curse-Talk*. There's a whole world out there that's fine with you failing to succeed. Why rob yourself of the one true cheerleader you have – yourself? Every time you go on a *Self-Curse-Talk* rampage you desecrate a higher part of yourself. The real danger is that people don't understand that this type of internal monologue is nothing more than internalized negative emotions, feelings and beliefs that aren't necessarily true. But if they *believe* they are true, that's all that matters in their world. As I said earlier, that thing called your *subconscious mind* does not know the difference between true or false. It only knows the information that's programmed into it. People all over this planet have created belief systems that will create nothing but negative and destructive consequences."

"So, people unconsciously use their mind to create negative false truths that keep them from the very things that they desire?" Bernie asks.

"Yes," Bob says. "For the most part, they are not aware of what they're doing to themselves. Not only do they not know that what they think is what they get, they also have no idea that what they say out loud during troubling times will have even a greater impact, because the words you speak out loud amplify your feelings and trigger mental images."

"So, if what you think is what you get, then what you say out loud is what you ask for?"

"Exactly." Bob mimics a person driving up to a fast-food drive-thru speaker. "Uh, yeah, I'll have the Super Failure Mega Combo, uh, large, and a side of self-loathing."

The Big Mouth Inside Your Head

"Well, what do I have to do to get my life to work for me and not against me?" Bernie asks.

"You have to stop The Big Mouth voice track!"

"My second wife? What does she have to do with this?"

Bob laughs. "No, Bernie. Not your second wife. I'm talking about The Big Mouth inside your head."

"Ha! That's exactly my second wife! She's always in my head yapping away!"

Bob shakes his head. "The Big Mouth is what most people would call *The Ego*. Some even call it *The Devil*, which is a little melodramatic, but if you listen to it there will be hell to pay. It's the voice that feeds off of your deep-rooted fears." Again, Bob does a spot-on Bernie. *"'What if I don't have enough money?' 'What if I fail?' 'I knew this would happen!' 'What if…'"*

"Okay! Okay, Bob! I get your point!"

"Do you really? Bernie, The Big Mouth is a great deceiver. Its mission is to keep your toxic beliefs alive. Every day The Big Mouth has only one agenda, which is to create stories that will convince you that you can't and won't achieve the success and happiness you desire. This is the main reason why your life isn't working."

"So, The Big Mouth was probably responsible for me not seeing the seed possibility of a prayer being answered?"

"Yes. For the most part, it was. No matter how intense your troubles, it's always fear-based thoughts, beliefs built from past experiences and from the negative words you use, that result in the loss of control of your emotions. When you lose control of your emotions, you eventually lose control of the situation. This leaves you feeling defeated and hopeless."

Bernie sits up straight and yanks at the lapels of his jacket. "You know, Bob, I have a pretty big mouth myself. Why don't I just tell this big-son-of-a…? Why don't I just tell The BM to get lost, that this is my life? I'm in control here!"

Bob seems delighted with the fire Bernie is showing. "Now you're talking, Bernie! That's exactly what you should do!"

Bernie seems surprised. "It is?"

"It sure as *Hellmann's* is! The best way to take control is to stop worrying and complaining about your plight and start talking back to this pain in the ass in your head."

Bernie grins. "Bob, please. Your language."

"Not now, Bernie, I'm on a roll! Talk back to that voice that's articulating the defeatist language invading your brain and is taking a direct verbal pass out into the world. *'Here we go again. Why is this happening to me? Why can't I ever get a break? I will never be able to handle this. Good things never happen to me. What's the use? No one cares anyway.'* These words and the devastating emotions they elicit are not only self-defeating in the moment, but they can create a lifetime of serious consequences. *Self-Curse-Talk* can stifle creativity and productivity and keep you from seeing possibilities to a brighter outcome or finding solutions to problems." Bob looks to make sure Bernie is on board. "The good news is that once you recognize...*once you become aware of*...the dismal reality that these thoughts and words create for yourself, you can step back, observe the direction you are going in and take action against them. You do this by counterattacking with empowering emotional thoughts and words that instill love, faith, confidence, courage and determination that will eventually make you feel better."

> *"Awareness is the key that will set you free from the Big Mouth inside your head. Can I hear a 'Hallelujah!?' Sorry, I get a little carried away sometimes."*
>
> *– Bob*

"So, as soon as I recognize or 'become aware' that I'm not feeling right or of the negative reality I'm creating, I shift my way of thinking to empowering thoughts and words."

"Yes," says Bob. "But you must first become aware that you are not feeling right...that there is some sort of emotional duress in your world. It's also being aware that you have a choice in how to deal with it and, more importantly, how to respond. Most people go through life with no idea that their negative thoughts and emotions are steering the course of their lives, often in the opposite direction of where they want to go."

"I see." Bernie nods while stroking his chin. "If you're not aware that your own choices are really what's happening to you, it's impossible to choose a better way to respond."

"Exactly," says Bob. "Whatever it is that is bringing you down, acknowledge the fear-based feeling it represents and immediately go on the offensive and bombard those feelings with emotionally charged words that elicit confidence, courage and faith. The more emotionally charged your words are, the more effect they will have."

Bernie jumps in on Bob's enthusiasm. "Because those emotionally charged words are a direct connection to you…to your energy field."

"Right!" says Bob. "And if you're worried about someone catching you talking to yourself and thinking you're crazy, just hop in the car or take a walk and give that voice in your head a piece of your mind. Oh…one more thing. Have fun with this! Unleash your Humor Being! Use your imagination! Do it in a funny voice or your favorite impression!"

Bernie stands up from his chair. "You mean like this?" He tries and fairly succeeds in speaking with the voice of Megatron from the *Transformers* movies: *"Hey, Big Mouth! I know you're there, and I know what you're trying to do. But it won't work! Because I'm in control here! Do you understand? I AM IN CONTROL!"* Bernie begins walking robotically around Bob's office. "I choose what thoughts flow through my mind! I get to choose the words that are coming out of my mouth! And I get to choose how I feel in any situation! And guess what, Mr. Big Mouth? I am the radiating center of success and abundance!" Bernie robot-walks over behind Bob's desk and puts a hand on his shoulder. "But most of all, I have a force, a friend named Bob that is bigger than anything you can throw at me! So, go ahead! Hit me with your best shot, Big Mouth! One thing is certain – I will prevail! No matter how many times you try to control my life…I will prevail! I've got my shift together!"

Bob rises and gives him the standing ovation his performance deserves.

"Bernie! Bernie! Bernie!" Bob says. "Do you see how empowering and emotionally charged those words are? And how they can lift your spirits and propel you to move forward? Especially if you're having fun!"

"Yes! I really feel emotionally charged, and being a big, bad-ass robot from outer space helped to sell it!"

"Of course, you feel charged. Whether positive or negative, your words and the emotions behind them inevitably affect the way you feel, your attitude and, thus, your situation."

"And as soon as I open my mouth, I start that process in motion."

"*Exactly*. The more confident your thoughts and words are, the more confident you will feel. That's what gives you hope and enables you to see a higher outcome and even miracles."

"I get it now. Sometimes miracles occur simply by shifting your perception. I once read a quote from a guy named Wayne Dyer," Bernie recalls. "'When I change the way I look at things, then the things I look at will change.'"

"Yep, Wayne was right on target as usual. When adversity strikes, it is your perception of yourself and the world around you that are key factors to ensure your well-being. If the words you speak aloud reflect weakness, inadequacy or victimization, then the energy you send out will mirror those same qualities."

"And I can create miracles if the words I speak elicit emotions that reflect courage, power and a view of life that is a never-ending adventure and learning experience," Bernie says.

"Now who's on a roll?" says Bob.

"When life gets hard and things don't go as planned, what I say out loud will cause me to either resent it or surrender to it."

Bob claps his hands. "The surrender you're referring to involves letting go and yielding to something greater within you!"

"Once again, let go and let *you* take over."

"It's my job! Simply ask me to show you the way. Don't say, '*Oh Bob, I want this specific job opportunity or this particular person to come into my life.*' Instead, ask me to release your creative potential and for the right opportunity to fulfill it. Let go and trust that it will happen." Bob pulls out the briefcase again and starts packing more things from the desk into it. "Ask what needs to change in your life. Who do you need to forgive or what shift in perception needs to be made?"

Bob pulls ordinary bubble wrap from his desk drawer and carefully rolls the hourglass up.

"Don't ever be afraid to ask me to heal your life," he says. "For whatever you have done, it will always be forgiven. ALWAYS! I don't want to brag, well…maybe just a little…but I am greater than any disappointment, mistake or screw-up you can make. I am the *Great Bounce-Back Factor*. No matter how many times you fall, I will always be there to pick you up and, if necessary, carry you, as I have done so many times before."

Bob places the hourglass gingerly into the briefcase. "Through me you can always start again. All you have to do is to acknowledge my presence – my energy – *that is within you*, meet me halfway and believe." Bob also tosses the globe and water glass (still half full) into the briefcase. "Bernie, my dear friend, I ask you to ask me for these things so you can achieve the success and happiness you so much deserve. Abundance, success, wealth, happiness and the manifestations of your dreams are there for the taking, but you will experience only that which you take into your consciousness. Therefore, any limitation must be a limitation in thought and the faith that shapes that which you desire. In every challenging experience you face at work or in life, there is always a time when problems exist merely as seed possibilities. Do not allow those seed possibilities to take root. That's your job."

Bob flicks his fingers, and the levitating chalk appears from nowhere to zoom into the case.

"Remember," he continues, "your thought is your life, and all lack and financial problems begin in the mind. Whenever you feel concern, fear or worry about relationships, money, work or success, say 'no!' to The Big Mouth inside your head and say 'yes!' to your Higher Self and to the abundance that is your right to claim. Tell The BM, as you call it, to get behind you. Stand up to this deceiving voice and declare that it's not real, even though it may seem like it's real. When you deny this Ego-driven voice, you bring forth me. With us together, The Big Mouth literally doesn't have a prayer of being heard."

Bernie stands finally. "Together we are the Dynamic Duo!"

"You got that right!"

Bob and Bernie high-five each other.

"This wonderful world is at your command. The answer to your prayers can come at any time, from anywhere. All you have to do is BELIEVE, TAKE POSITIVE ACTION, KEEP YOUR EYES, EARS… AND HEART…OPEN." Bob plucks the stapler from the desk and holds it out for a moment. "Even if you do everything right, you're guaranteed to fail sometimes. That's how it is." He snaps the stapler shut towards Bernie a few times as if it's a crab claw. "When that happens, just try and keep it together." With that, he stuffs the stapler into the briefcase and snaps it shut.

All becomes silent, as if a billion doors also closed in unison across the universe.

B⬤B's

High Points to Remember

*I*n any given circumstance, you have the power to use your mind to create feel-good thoughts that will propel you to view any situation from a higher part of yourself – from an advantage rather than a disadvantage. The more you do this, the more you solidify a healthier belief system."

*E*very time you go on a **Self-Curse-Talk** *rampage you desecrate a higher part of yourself. The real danger is that people don't understand that this type of internal monologue is nothing more than internalized negative emotions, feelings and beliefs that aren't necessarily true. But if they **believe** they are true, that's all that matters in their world."*

*T*he Big Mouth inside your head is what most people would call **The Ego**. Some even call it **The Devil**, which is a little melodramatic, but if you listen to it there will be hell to pay. It's the voice that feeds off of your deep-rooted fears."

16

The L Word

> *"Your greatest power is to show love, to receive love and to be love."*
>
> **— OPRAH WINFREY**

*B*ernie stands, looking at Bob, shifting back and forth from one foot to the other in anticipation of some yet-unseen event. "Is that it? Are we through?"

Bob is standing, briefcase in hand. "No. There's one more thing, Bernie…This is crucial…This is why I saved it for last."

The smile fades from Bernie's face. He can see that Bob has become very serious. "I'm listening."

"Although your thoughts, beliefs, attitude, imagination, visualization, feelings, faith, attention and intention and everything else we discussed are important ingredients to create the life you desire, it is crucial that you understand the most important ingredient of all. For without this most important ingredient the actualization of your desires will not manifest to their highest, fullest potential, if at all."

"Okay."

"This is the greatest manifestation secret in the world that most people leave by the wayside."

"Okay."

"In fact, without this ingredient, life would be without joy… without meaning. I daresay humanity would not exist."

"Okay."

"This is the foundation you must build your entire life on. For, as you well know, when you are striving to build the life you desire, things don't always go the way you want. In fact, sometimes it will seem that your whole world is falling apart piece by piece, but you can always rebuild on a strong foundation. I can't stress this enough…"

Bernie finally explodes. *"Come on, Bob! You're killing me here! What is it? What's the most important ingredient?"*

Bob reaches out and touches Bernie's shoulder. "Here's a hint. It's the most powerful four-letter word you can speak during your time on Earth." Seeing that Bernie might be going a different direction, Bob quickly says, "Love."

"Love?"

"Yes. Love is the most powerful force in the universe. Love is the best way to get to know me. Love is what I am and who I am. And because you are my creation, Love is what you are and who you are. Do you understand what I mean when I say Love?"

"I think you'd better explain in more detail, because in my experience, it hasn't been all that it's cracked up to be. Apparently, there is more to Love than what I've been led to believe."

"That's very wise of you, Bernie. Contrary to what most people think, Love is more than a feeling. It's a state of being. Love is your true nature, but because you're programmed by the stuff of the world, you can only define yourself by what you do and not who you truly are. In other words, you can never be more like me than when you first Love yourself, all human beings, and when you enjoy and truly Love the process of whatever you are trying to achieve – unconditionally – regardless of your circumstances."

"So, Love is the key ingredient to life?"

"Yes, but you can't force Love. You can't manipulate it to get something. You Love for Love's sake. True Love is its own reward. The word *unconditional* is key."

"Why?"

"Imagine yourself back at the foot of Mt. Rainier. You're captivated by its splendor. You feel the warmth of the sun, smell the fragrance from the pine and array of flowers. You seek shade under a tree or shelter in a cave and quench your thirst from a mountain stream. Notice how nature offers all of its splendor indiscriminately to every living thing. In other words, imagine the sun as being biased and thinking it will offer its warmth and energy only to those who are worthy even though it has never met you. Or a flower deciding it will reveal its fragrance only to those who praise and respect its beauty. By its very nature, a tree or a cave will always offer its shade and protection to all people, animals and living things. Oceans, rivers, lakes and mountain streams will offer their essence to even those who contaminate and destroy them."

"If you can contemplate and comprehend the ways in which nature is always offering itself unconditionally to all living things, without judgment, without asking for anything in return, you will have a profound understanding of what true Love is."

"To Love is to live. To live is to Love," Bernie says.

"I Love when you recap things concisely like that," Bob says.

Bernie stands for a moment, eyes closed, and thinks about the power of Love. Finally, he speaks. "So, whenever I am praying or creating my new Shifting habits, I should first and foremost come from a foundation of Love. Everything should evolve and revolve around a state of Love."

"Absolutely. Don't get me wrong. You can heal and transform your life with positive thoughts and powerful beliefs, but in the hierarchy of everything, Love is the most powerful catalyst of all."

"What you're saying is that Love is the supreme magnetic force," Bernie says.

"Magnetic, quantum, theoretical, literal. Yes. When your thoughts and beliefs are coming from a foundation of Love, you are super-charging your connection to my energy field. When you visualize your desire with Love, and when your goals are motivated by Love, you have the highest chance of manifestation. Always remember, Bernie, you are always in co-creation with me. Therefore, Love is the single most valuable thing you can give that is in harmony with me."

"Because you are Love and Love is you."

"And because you are also Love and Love is you. Once again, John and Paul were right."

"The Apostles?"

"No, the Beatles. *'All you need is Love.'* The key is to be vigilant about keeping your Love light burning. Your success, your happiness, your relationship with others and with life in general are determined by the relationship you have with yourself in any given moment. In other words, the relationship you have with yourself steers the course of your life in every situation, event and circumstance. Bernie, you have to Love yourself before you can ever expect to Love anyone or anything else."

> *"Love...Love...Love...I absolutely Love that word!"*
>
> *– Bob*

"How do I keep my Love light burning, especially when times are tough? I mean, we've already agreed that some people have a lot to deal with."

"By being eternally grateful for what you have. Every day, throughout the day, bless the things life has given you rather than cursing what life hasn't given you. Continually ask yourself, *'How can I serve? What can I do today to make the world a better place?'* Display acts of kindness to everyone and everything, including yourself. Learn to forgive others as well as yourself, regardless of the circumstances.

Practice loving those who have intentionally hurt you. Try to walk a mile in their shoes. Respect others' points of view. Try not to view arguments and disagreements simply as being right or wrong, but rather as a matter of advantages and disadvantages for all involved. Treat life as a game. Unleash the child within you and have fun. Know that your sense of humor is your sense of perspective. Every day, Bernie, throughout the day, find the laughter within and around you. All of these things and so much more encompass Love. When you are able to instill these qualities into yourself, in all people and in all things, you not only attract Love, you become Love, and Love becomes you."

Bernie feels a tickle at the sides of his mouth and is surprised to find he has been crying.

Bob continues. "Incorporating these qualities may seem difficult at first, especially during challenging times when your emotions get in the way. That's when you have to really be aware of The Big Mouth."

"It's amazing how much power The BM has," says Bernie.

"What's even more amazing is the power *you allow* The Big Mouth to have, and even more amazing is the realization that The Big Mouth is a part of you. Its main mission is to keep your toxic labels alive and create stories that will convince you that you cannot achieve success and enjoy the moment. Strange that two goals can exist within the same body, no?"

"One hell of a way to live, isn't it?"

"There is no way you can achieve happiness, much less peace, amidst so much chatter that accompanies this annoying and controlling voice inside your head," Bob explains.

"I guess my job is to keep my ego or The Big Mouth inside my head from taking control."

Bob continues. "That's right. But the fact is, life becomes easier when you push your ego-based thoughts and emotions aside and surrender every aspect of your life to your Higher Self. That's me, however you want to define me. Once you incorporate the *Shifting Habits* and *Common Sense Success Strategies* that I explained earlier, your connection to me will become more empowering, and The Big Mouth will begin to lose its influence on you."

Bob steps back and pulls a hat from the coat rack at the back of the office, plopping it on before he turns to speak again. "Use your choices wisely. What you think you want may not necessarily be what you need to be truly happy and successful. More often than not, what you want feeds the Ego. When you fulfill your needs, you feed your Soul. Every now and then, pause for just a moment and ask yourself, 'Which one am I feeding right now?'"

Bob pats the briefcase at his side.

"Choose wisely, Bernie, because time has a cruel way of saying 'I told you so.' Use your Wand properly. May the *SHIFT* always be with you, my dear friend."

Bernie is filled with Love, though he still finds tears streaming down his face.

"Holy Shift!" he croaks.

"Holy indeed!" says Bob.

"Thank you!! Thank you. I really don't know what else to say… Thank you, Bob. I'm at a loss for words."

"It's okay. I know exactly what you're thinking."

Bernie rolls his eyes. "I wish you wouldn't do that."

"Sorry." Bob grins. "It's a habit. Sometimes I just can't help myself knowing everything."

Bernie stands for several seconds, looking at Bob, taking it all in. "So, is this it? This is the end of our conversation? We can't talk like this anymore?"

"Bernie, it's time for you to go back to your physical body and live your life the way you're supposed to. You can always talk to me. Anytime, anywhere. I will always listen. ALWAYS! And although you will no longer see me or hear me in the way you do now, you can see and hear me through the deeds, happenings and manifestations of others. Just experience the world around you, Bernie. When you are captivated by a scenic view or a glorious work of art, you will see me. When you hear the sounds of people laughing with joy in their hearts, you will hear me. As you listen to birds calling to one another, also hear my Love call to you. There is absolutely no limit to the variety of ways I can communicate with you. Your part is to be attentive to my messages."

Bob pauses for a brief moment.

"You can also find me in tragedy and people filled with grief. For I can take the deepest sorrow and transform it into the highest good. When you witness others overcoming extreme adversity, you will know the miraculous power of me. When you observe those who are struggling, you will see the teacher in me, and so it will always be. All of life goes on within me and around me. And within and around you."

Bernie is overwhelmed. *What do you say to Bob himself when he plucks you from the jaws of death and gives you a second chance?* he thinks.

"Thank you! Thank you, Bob! I will make you proud! I promise! I will make these strategies a habit! And when I see you again, hopefully in a long, long…long time, I look forward to seeing a highlight reel of all the opportunities I recognized by being in the moment and connected to my Higher Power! "And Bob?" Bernie utters, his voice cracking and full of emotion.

"Yes?"

"I Love you."

Bob smiles, opens his arms and draws Bernie close to him in a Love-filled embrace. There, they become one luminous entity, a melding of human and spirit.

"Bobspeed, my friend," says Bob as he, the room and Bernie vanish into darkness, leaving a small dot of brilliant white light behind.

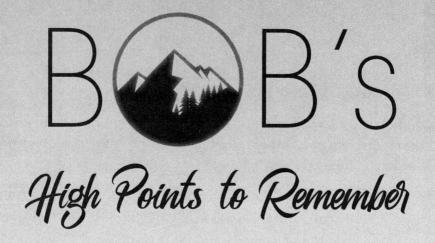

BOB's
High Points to Remember

*L*ove is the most powerful force in the universe. Love is the best way to get to know me. Love is what I am and who I am. And because you are my creation, Love is what you are and who you are."

*W*hen you visualize your desire with Love, and when your goals are motivated by Love, you have the highest chance of manifestation."

*A*lways remember, you are always in co-creation with me. Therefore, Love is the single most valuable thing you can give that is in harmony with me."

*T*he relationship you have with yourself steers the course of your life in every situation, event and circumstance. In other words, you have to Love yourself before you can ever expect to Love anyone or anything else."

Epilogue

BERNIE MERRIT WAS WHISTLING ALONG WITH THE BEATLES as *All You Need Is Love* poured through the speakers in the private car that had become his mode of transportation to and from the airport. He began to tap his toes to the music. He didn't need his toes for anything else since his usual driver, Charlie, was behind the wheel, and was trapped in a seemingly endless parking lot of cars on the Long Island Expressway. Bernie was giving a speech in New York City, which was fifty miles from his home on Long Island, and I-495 was still the best route even with the bumper-to-bumper traffic. When he heard the song, he thought to himself, *Huh, nice coincidence,* but then caught himself declaring out loud, *"Coincidence is just Bob's way of remaining anonymous."*

Charlie just nodded his head in agreement, as he had gotten used to hearing Bernie make such pronouncements, especially prior to a speaking engagement.

Three years had passed since his *"heart event,"* and as he sat contemplating how his presentation was going to go, he tapped out the rhythm of the song on the fashionable briefcase that was perched on the passenger seat next to him. It was almost like Morse code, a constant thumping of his fingers on the smooth leather, as if he was sending a signal to some far distant operator.

Bernie had awakened from his intervention with a new attitude towards life. Shortly after his experience, he decided to leave behind the golden handcuffs that had locked him into a corporate job that had been sucking precious energy out of him. His former co-workers all chipped in to give him a really nice briefcase and presented it to him on his last day at the office, and he felt unnaturally comforted by it. He felt like it was a symbol of the newfound realization that he had more control over his life than he had ever known, and more to give than he could possibly have imagined.

Bernie had found his voice and brought forth his *Humor Being* to the masses in a big way, as an inspirational speaker, exchanging his desk for the stage and desk phone for a microphone. He also had become an author, recounting his near-death experiences in *The Bob Factor*, which flew off the shelves in record numbers and landed the book on several best-seller lists.

Bernie had never felt better in his life.

While he still spent time on airplanes and in hotels, the reasons for his travel had changed dramatically, and the positive side effects of his new path were evident. He'd lost that extra weight, and his eyes and conscience were clear from being on stage, reminding people of the best within themselves, which, in turn, had transformed him as well.

He even rolled down the window on the car and yelled "I LOVE YOUR TRUCK, DUDE!" at a guy who was driving a massive F-350 pickup, who cut Charlie off, who then proceeded to flip him off. Bernie gave the guy a thumbs-up, which simply confused the fella, who hurriedly rolled up his window. Bernie just laughed it off, a very different reaction than in the past, when he would have returned the middle finger salute.

Once at the parking garage, the line was long, and the attendant wasn't very engaged. When the big car finally pulled up, Bernie asked the man in the small glass booth if he could park here by the decade instead of by the hour, as his presentation might end up taking longer than expected.

A slow smile spread across the attendant's face. He wasn't used to a sense of humor, and it made his day better. "Have a nice day," the man said.

"You can count on it!" said Bernie enthusiastically. "I'll see you later, Charlie." Then he jumped out of the car.

While traffic had him running a bit late, it really didn't bother him. Ever since he had set out on his new course, Bernie just didn't seem to care as much as he used to about the things that had made him anxious and angry. He whistled as he checked in with the building security, signed his name, took his badge and waited patiently as the woman at the desk dialed three wrong numbers to verify his appointment as the keynote speaker at the conference.

On the elevator ride up to the tower conference room, Bernie thought briefly about his conversation with Bob three years ago, which felt like it happened yesterday, as the illusion of time tends to have that effect. "Enjoy the moment, regardless of your circumstances," Bob had said. "It's the only way to do anything." Bernie smiled. Bob's words were an ongoing reminder that everything *always* works out, in *all-ways*.

When the elevator doors opened, he strode calmly down the hall, pushed open the giant oak double-doors, and there he found a crowd of five hundred people that were creating an incredible buzz of anticipation, many of them already purchasing a copy of his book so they could get them autographed at the conclusion of the talk.

In short order, they took their seats, the emcee of the event made a quick introduction. Bernie stepped onto the stage, tapped the microphone on his lapel and said, "If you're happy and you know it clap your hands…"

The audience immediately responded by clapping loudly, the sound echoing off the walls in the room.

With a smile on his face, Bernie continued, "Just checking…just checking…*just… checking.*"

The roomful of people burst out in laughter, then leaned back in their chairs with great anticipation of what was sure to be a powerful message.

"Good morning, everyone! So, I was almost late for my own presentation, but time is a strange thing. You think you have it. Then you lose it, then you realize all you have is *this very* moment."

Bernie then carefully pulled an hourglass from the briefcase and set it gingerly in front of him before tossing the briefcase aside. He cleared his throat, grinning like a man who had just won the lottery. He smiled, took a deep breath and said, "Thirty-six months ago, I had a heart attack. Matter of fact, I died on the operating table. Only then did I truly come to know how important my life is."

Bernie flipped the hourglass, and the sand began marking time in a most ancient way. For the next ninety minutes, Bernie shared all that he had learned about the importance of the *choices* we make and the *chances* we take. He drilled home that *wake-up calls* can lead to a serious *shift in direction* – if we pay *attention* to our *intention*. He had the room in the palm of his hand when insisting that in order to become a better *Human Being*, we must bring forth our inner *Humor Being*. He spoke his truth with a fervor and conviction that had long been dormant. The room had become a vortex of infectious, clear, healing energy.

Finally, Bernie simply said, "There is no 'secret.' Life is really very simple. *All you need is Love.*"

The crowd leapt to their feet, a rousing standing ovation filled the space with applause, and Bernie let the vibration wash over him.

He sat for a long time at the book table, as people lined up to thank him for sharing his message, many of them saying, *"It was as if you were here just for me today."*

Bernie signed each and every book as if it was written for the person standing in front of him, and, in so many ways, it was. Finally, the line was gone, the room was empty, and Bernie sat for a few moments to let the experience soak in a bit. He took a glance at his watch and realized more than three hours had passed quickly.

Then, slowly, he began to pack up, putting the hourglass and notes back into his briefcase. Just as he was about to leave, Bernie noticed a man in the back corner of the room starting to clean up and put chairs away.

He was tall, with a long ponytail, wearing faded jeans, a button-down shirt and earbuds, going about his business seemingly oblivious to what had just taken place. The man turned and gave a thumbs-up, putting a broad smile on Bernie's face.

Just a few minutes later, Bernie was making his way out of the elevator in the garage. He jumped in the waiting black car and said, "Okay, Charlie, let's hit the road, my friend."

Bernie could tell immediately there was different driver behind the wheel. He was a big, burly man with rosy cheeks, thinning white hair and a perpetual smile. Bernie thought, if he had a long white beard, he'd be the perfect Santa Claus.

"Mr. Merrit," the driver said, "Charlie had to make a pickup at the airport. I'll be driving you home today, sir."

His voice was vaguely familiar.

"Well, alrighty then," Bernie said. "Thanks for filling in for Charlie. I appreciate it."

"No problem, Mr. Merrit, and forgive me for gushing, sir, but I am one of your biggest fans. I watched you on *Ellen* last week and went out and bought your book the very next day."

"Wow. Thanks very much for doing that.

"Matter of fact, I have the book with me. Any chance you might sign it for me, sir?"

"Of course, of course."

With that, the man turned around and passed *The Bob Factor* to Bernie, who reached inside his jacket pocket for a pen.

"How would you like me to sign it?" Bernie asked.

"Well, my name is Robert, but my friends call me...*Bob*."

"Bob! I love that name!" Bernie quipped.

"If you could sign it '*To my good friend Bob, with best wishes,*' I would really appreciate it, Mr. Merrit. After reading your book, I feel like I've known you forever."

Bernie stared inquisitively at the man.

As he signed the book, a soft light seemed to illuminate the car. Bernie slowly handed the book back, and they rode in silence to his condo.

When the car pulled into the driveway, Bob turned around and said, "Mr. Merrit, it's been an honor to drive you, sir."

Bernie looked directly into Bob's smiling face and said, "Please, call me Bernie. After all...we are friends...forever, right?"

Bob laughed. "Absolutely. I hope our paths cross again soon."

Bernie was still a bit confounded by the way his day was ending, thanked the driver and reached in his wallet for a tip.

"Oh, Mr. Merrit...uh...*Bernie*...please, no tip, sir. I have gained so much from reading your book. It's truly a blessing...*and so are you.* That's more than enough."

Bernie slowly put his wallet back, nodded to Robert, who exited the car and made his way to the passenger door. He opened it up, and the two men stood eye to eye for a moment.

"You know, Bernie," Robert said, "I was thinking on the ride back here how important it is to stay awake in life rather than needing a life-changing event to *change our lives.* But, perhaps, as you said in your presentation this morning, 'There is no secret. Life is really very simple. *All you need is Love.*'"

"Uh...*yes*...but, Robert..."

"Please...*call me Bob...*"

"*Touché.*" Bernie smiled, then continued. "*Bob,* how did you know that's what I said to close my talk this morning? Were you in the room?"

"Well...I guess you could say that..."

Robert extended his hand. Instinctively, Bernie reached out, met his grip and, in an instant, felt a familiar energy rush through him, as time seemed to stand still.

After a moment, they moved apart, and Bernie started to make his way to the entrance of his house. Just before he could open the door, his cell phone rang. The caller ID read "Charlie."

"Mr. Merrit, so glad I reached you! I am not sure what happened. I decided to go get a quick bite to eat while you were doing your presentation and must have lost track of time. I received a text from the company you were due to be picked up from 30 minutes ago, but when I got there you were gone. Did you take an Uber or taxi? I am so very sorry."

"No worries, Charlie. The company sent another driver. I just got home."

"Another driver? *That's not possible,* Mr. Merrit. There are only four of us on call today, and I was having lunch with the three other drivers when I got the pickup reminder."

Bernie quickly turned around and caught sight of the Town Car making a left turn at the light down the block. Ignoring Charlie's voice on the phone, he jogged a few steps towards the street. Just as the car completed its turn, he could hear Bob singing "All you need is love…*dot da dada da…*"

He shouted, "Robert! *Bob*! Wait…*wait!*"

Just a split second before the car vanished from sight, Bernie caught a glimpse of the license plate...